Dr Dobson
Answers Your Questions
about
Raising Children

JAMES DOBSON

KINGSWAY PUBLICATIONS
EASTBOURNE

ISBN 0 86065 526 1

The publishers wish to express their
gratitude to Hodder & Stoughton Limited
for permission to reproduce material based
on and quoted from *Hide or Seek*.

Printed in Great Britain for
KINGSWAY PUBLICATIONS LTD
Lottbridge Drove, Eastbourne, E. Sussex BN23 6NT by
Anchor Brendon Ltd, Tiptree, Essex

This book is affectionately dedicated to the professional colleagues and staff members who help me direct the activities of our nonprofit ministry, Focus on the Family. Paul Nelson, Gil Moegerle, Peb Jackson, Rolf Zettersten, Mike Trout, and 360 other coworkers and friends are deeply devoted to the principles and values expressed throughout this book.

It is entirely appropriate, therefore, that I take this opportunity to thank them for their diligent efforts to preserve the institution of the family.

Acknowledgments

It is with gratitude that I hereby acknowledge the assistance of four women who contributed significantly to the production of this book. They are *Virginia Muir,* Senior Editor at Tyndale House Publishers, who assembled original material from my prior writings and recordings; *Dee Otte,* my Administrative Assistant, who kept the wheels turning when they would otherwise have ground to a halt; *Teresa Kvisler,* who typed and collated the final manuscript; and, of course, my beloved wife, *Shirley,* who is an active partner in everything I do. Without the encouragement and dedication of these four members of the "team," a half-finished manuscript would remain hopelessly buried beneath a mountain of paper on my desk.

CONTENTS

INTRODUCTION

THE ETERNAL SOURCE

When a child was born during the 1800s or before, his inexperienced mother was assisted by many friends and relatives who hovered around to offer their advice and support. Very few of these aunts and grandmothers and neighbors had ever read a book on child-rearing, but that was no handicap. They possessed a certain folk wisdom which gave them confidence in handling babies and children. They had a prescribed answer for every situation, whether it proved to be right or wrong. Thus, a young woman was systematically taught how to "mother" by older women who had many years' experience in caring for little people.

With the disappearance of this "extended family," however, the job of motherhood became more frightening. Many young couples today do not have access to such supportive relatives and friends. They live in a mobile society wherein the next-door neighbors are often total strangers. Furthermore, their own mothers and fathers may live in faraway Detroit or Dallas or Portland (and might not be trusted even if they were available to help). Consequently, young parents often experience great anxieties over their lack of preparation for raising children. Dr. Benjamin Spock described their fears in this way: "I can remember mothers who cried on the morning they were to take their baby home. 'I won't know what to do,' they wailed."

This anxiety has brought parents rushing to the "experts" for information and advice. They have turned to pediatricians, psychologists, psychiatrists and educators for answers to their questions about the complexities of parenthood. Therefore, increasing numbers of American children have been reared according to this professional consultation during the past forty years. In fact, no country on earth has embraced the teachings of child psychology and the offerings of family specialists more than has the United States.

It is now appropriate that we ask, "What has been the effect of this professional influence?" One would expect that the mental health of our children would exceed that of individuals raised in nations not having this technical assistance. Such has not been the case. Juvenile delinquency, drug abuse, alcoholism, unwanted pregnancies, mental illness, and suicide are rampant among the young, and continue their steady rise. In many ways, we have made a mess of parenthood! Of course, I would not be so naive as to blame all these woes on the bad advice of the "experts," but I believe they have played a role in creating the problem. Why? *Because in general, behavioral scientists have lacked confidence in the Judeo-Christian ethic and have disregarded the wisdom of this priceless tradition!*

It appears to me that the twentieth century has spawned a generation of professionals who felt qualified to ignore the parental attitudes and practices of more than 2,000 years, substituting instead their own wobbly-legged insights of the moment. Each authority, writing from his own limited experience and reflecting his own unique biases, has sold us his guesses and suppositions as though they represented Truth itself. One anthropologist, for example, wrote an incredibly gallish article in *The Saturday Evening Post*, November 1968, entitled "We Scientists Have a Right to Play God." Dr. Edmund Leach stated,

> There can be no source for these moral judgments except the scientist himself. In traditional religion, morality was held to derive from God, but God was only credited with the authority to establish and enforce moral rules because He was also credited with supernatural powers of creation and destruction. Those powers have now been usurped by man, and he must take on the moral responsibility that goes with them.

That paragraph summarizes the many ills of our day. Arrogant men like Edmund Leach have argued God out of existence and put themselves in His exalted place. Armed with that authority, they have issued their ridiculous opinions to the public with unflinching confidence. In turn, desperate families grabbed their porous recommendations like life preservers, which often sank to the bottom, taking their passengers down with them.

These false teachings have included the notions that loving discipline is damaging, irresponsibility is healthy, religious instruction is hazardous, defiance is a valuable ventilator of anger, all authority is dangerous, and on and on it goes. In more recent years, this humanistic perspective has become even more extreme and anti-Christian. For example, one mother told me recently that she works in a youth project which has obtained the consultative services of a certain psychologist. He has been teaching the parents of the kids in the program that in order for young girls to grow up with more healthy attitudes toward sexuality, their fathers should have intercourse with them when they are twelve years of age. If you gasped at that suggestion, be assured that it shocked me also. Yet this is where moral relativism leads—this is the ultimate product of a human endeavor which accepts no standards, honors no cultural values, acknowledges no absolutes, and serves no "god" except the human mind. King Solomon wrote about such foolish efforts in Proverbs 14:12: "There is a way that *seemeth* right unto a man, but the end thereof are the ways of death."

Now admittedly, the book you are about to read also contains many suggestions and perspectives which I have not attempted to validate or prove. How do my writings differ from the unsupported recommendations of those whom I have criticized? The distinction lies in the *source* of the views being presented. The underlying principles expressed herein are not my own innovative insights which would be forgotten in a brief season or two. Instead, they originated with the inspired biblical writers who gave us the foundation for all relationships in the home. As such, these principles have been handed down generation after generation to this very day. Our ancestors taught them to their children who taught them to their children, keeping the knowledge alive for posterity. Now, unfortunately, that understanding is being vigorously challenged in some circles and altogether forgotten in others.

If I have had a primary mission in writing this book, therefore, it has not been to earn royalty or propagate the name of James Dobson or demonstrate my professional skills. My purpose has been nothing more ambitious than to verbalize the Judeo-Christian tradition regarding the discipline of children and to apply those concepts to today's families. This approach has been deeply engrained in the Western culture but has never been expressly written, to my knowledge. It involves control with love, a reasonable introduction to self-discipline and responsibility, parental *leadership* which seeks the best interest of the child, respect for the dignity and worth of every member of the family, realistic boundaries that are enforced with confident firmness, and finally, a judicious use of rewards and punishment when required for training. It is a system that has existed for more than twenty centuries of parenthood. I did not invent it, nor can I change it. My task has been merely to report what I believe to be the prescription of the Creator Himself. And I am convinced that this understanding will remain viable for as long as mothers and fathers and children cohabit the face of the earth. It will certainly outlive humanism and the puny efforts of mankind to find an alternative.

SECTION 1

LIFE IN THE FAMILY

I'm afraid I'm not ready to raise the baby I bore last month. Sure, I understand how to feed and bathe and diaper him. But I'm uncertain about the future. What should be the objective of my relationship with him? Can you give me a foundational philosophy that will guide my parenting efforts during my child's first four years of life?

Your question reminds me of a friend who flew his single-engine airplane toward a small country airport some years ago. He arrived as the sun had dropped behind a mountain at the close of the day, and by the time he maneuvered into a position to land, he could not see the hazy field below. He had no lights on his plane and there was no one on duty at the airport. He circled the runway for another attempt to land, but the darkness had then become even more impenetrable. For two hours he flew his plane around and around in the blackness of the night, knowing that he faced certain death when his fuel was expended. Then, as greater panic gripped him, a miracle occurred. Someone on the ground heard the continuing drone of his engine and realized his predicament. That merciful man drove his car back and forth on the runway to show my friend the location of the airstrip, and then let his lights cast their beam from the far end while the plane landed.

I think of that story whenever I am coming down at night in a commercial airliner. As I look ahead, I can see the green lights bordering the runway which tell the captain where to direct the plane. If it stays between those lighted boundaries, all will be well. There is safety in that illuminated zone, but disaster lies to the left or right.

As new parents, we need clearly marked boundaries telling us where to steer the family ship. We require some guiding *principles*, as you requested, which will help us raise our children in safety and health.

Toward that end, let me provide two distinct messages which must be conveyed to every child during his first forty-eight months. These concepts are of great significance in my approach to parenthood, and can be thought of as beacons or guiding lights. They are:

1. "I love you more than you can possibly understand. You are precious to me and I thank God every day that He lets me raise you!"

2. "Because I love you, I must teach you to obey me. That is the only way I can take care of you and protect you from things that might hurt you. Let's read what the Bible tells us: 'Children, obey your parents, for this is what God wants you to do' (Eph. 6:1)." This is an abbreviated answer to a very important and complex question, but perhaps it will give you a place to begin formulating your *own* philosophy of parenting.[1]

Can you give us a guideline for how much work children should be given to do?

There should be a healthy balance between work and play. Many farm children of the past had daily chores that made life pretty difficult. Early in the morning and again after school they would feed the pigs, gather the eggs, milk the cows, and bring in the wood. Little time was reserved for fun, and childhood became a pretty drab experience. That was an extreme position and I certainly don't favor its return. However, contrast that level with its opposite, recommended by some modern behaviorists who recommend that we not even ask our children to water the lawn or let out the cat. According to this recommendation, Junior should be allowed to lie on his overfed stomach watching six or eight hours of worthless television while his schoolwork gathers dust in the corner. Both extremes, as usual, are harmful to the child. The logical middle ground can be found by giving the child an exposure to responsibility and work, but preserving time for his play and fun. The amount of time devoted to each activity should vary with the age of the child, gradually requiring more work as he grows older.[2]

Should parents force a child to eat?

No. I am no expert in nutrition, but I believe a normal child's appetite is governed by the amount of food he needs. He will get hungry when he needs nourishment. However, I do believe the parent should carefully guard that appetite, making sure that he satisfies it with the foods his body requires. A bit of sugar in the afternoon can make him disinterested in his dinner. Or he may sit down at the table and fill his stomach with juice or one item on his plate. Thus, it may be necessary to give him one kind of food at a time, beginning with iron-rich meat and other protein, followed by the less important items. Once he is satisfied, I can see no value in forcing him to continue eating. Incidentally, the parent should know that a child's appetite often drops off rapidly between two and three years of age. This occurs because his time of maximum growth rate has subsided, and his need for food is reduced.[3]

What do you think of the phrase "Children should be seen and not heard"?

That statement reveals a profound ignorance of children and their needs. I can't imagine how any loving adult could raise a vulnerable little boy or girl by that philosophy. Children are like clocks, they must be allowed to run![4]

Would you go so far as to apologize to a child if you felt you had been in the wrong?

I certainly would—and indeed, I have. A few years ago I was burdened with pressing responsibilities which made me fatigued and irritable. One particular evening I was especially grouchy and short-tempered with my ten-year-old daughter. I knew I was not being fair, but was simply too tired to correct my manner. Through the course of the evening, I blamed Danae for things that were not her fault and upset her needlessly several times. After going to bed, I felt bad about the way I had behaved and I decided to apologize the next morning. After a good night of sleep and a tasty breakfast, I felt much more optimistic about life. I approached my daughter before she left for school and said, "Danae, I'm sure you know that daddies are not perfect human beings. We get tired and irritable just like other people, and there are times when we are not proud of the way we behave. I know I wasn't fair with you last night. I was terribly grouchy, and I want you to forgive me."

Danae put her arms around me and shocked me down to my toes. She said, "I knew you were going to have to apologize, Daddy, and it's OK; I forgive you."

Can there be any doubt that children are often more aware of the struggles between generations than are their busy, harassed parents?[5]

I am very disappointed with the way my four-year-old is developing. If the present trends continue, he will be a failure as an adult. Is it possible to forecast a child's future character and personality traits from this early age?

Probably not. Rene Voeltzel said, "We must not look too soon in the child for the person he will later become." I agree. It is unfair and damaging to judge him too soon. Be patient and give your little fellow time to mature. Work gently on the traits that concern you the most, but, by all means, allow him the privilege of being a child. He will be one for such a brief moment, anyway.[6]

How do you feel about having a family council, where each member of the family has an equal vote on the decisions affecting the entire family?

It's a good idea to let each member of the family know that the others value his viewpoint and opinion. Most important decisions should be shared within the group because that is an excellent way to build fidelity and family loyalty. However, the equal vote idea is carrying the concept too far; an eight-year-old should not have the same influence that his mother and father have in making decisions. It should be clear to everyone that the parents are the benevolent captains of the ship.[7]

Should I punish my son for bed-wetting?

Absolutely not! It is never appropriate to punish a child for any involuntary action. To punish someone for something he simply cannot avoid doing is to set him up for serious problems.

Of course, if you have reason to think that your son is awake and simply lies there in bed and urinates because he is too lazy to get up and go to the bathroom, that is another matter. However, true enuresis is totally involuntary.[8]

Can you offer any advice for dealing with recurring bed-wetting in a six-year-old boy?

Enuresis can produce emotional and social distress for the older child. Thus, it is wise to help him conquer the problem as soon as possible. I would recommend that you make use of a buzzer device that emits a loud noise when your boy urinates at night. Sears, Roebuck and Co. sells a unit called a Wee Alert, which I have found effective *when used properly* for children four years of age and older.

Bed-wetting occurs in most cases as a result of very sound sleep, which makes it difficult, if not impossible, for the child to learn nighttime control on his own. His mind does not respond to the signal reflex action that ordinarily awakens a lighter sleeper. Fortunately, that reflex action can be trained or conditioned to awaken even a deep sleeper in most instances.

The Wee Alert system produces a very irritating sound when urination occurs at night. The child has been instructed to awaken one parent (determining which one can create some interesting marital arguments) who must place him in a tub of cool water or splash cold water on his face. Both alternatives are unpleasant, of course, but are essential to the success of the program. The child is told that this is *not* a form of punishment for wetting the bed. It is necessary to help him break the habit so he can invite friends to spend the night and he can go to other homes, as well. The cold water awakens the child fully and gives him a reason not to want to repeat the experience. It is a form of aversive conditioning, such as is used to help break the habit of smoking. Later, the relaxation immediately prior to urination is associated with the unpleasantness of the bell and the cold water. When that connection is made, urinary control is mastered.

This procedure may take from four to eight weeks to conquer bed-wetting, but success can occur much more quickly in some cases. My own son remained dry the third night we used the equipment. As indicated in the Wee Alert instructions, it is unnecessary to restrict liquids, get the child up at night, use punishment, etc. None of these standard procedures communicate with the unconscious mind during periods of deep, dreamy sleep. The Wee Alert system apparently does.

(Please note that I did not invent the Wee Alert system and receive no compensation from Sears for recommending this product. I merely suggest the device because it usually works.)

Another successful system is called a Nite-Train-r. It can be ordered from Nite-Train-r, P. O. Box 282, Newberg, OR 97132.[9]

My wife and I are extremely busy during this period of our lives. My job takes me on the road several days a week, and my wife has become very successful as a real estate agent. Quite honestly, we are not able to spend much time with our three children, but we give them our undivided attention when we are together. My wife and I wish we had more family time, but we take comfort in knowing that it's not the quantity of time between parent and child that really matters; it's the quality of that time that makes the difference. Would you agree with that statement?

There is a grain of truth in most popular notions, and this one is no exception. We can all agree that there is no benefit in being with our children seven days a week if we are angry, oppressive, unnurturing and capricious with them. But from that point forward, the quantity versus quality issue runs aground. Simply stated, *that dichotomy will not be tolerated in any other area of our lives; why do we apply it only to children?* Let me illustrate.

Let's suppose you are very hungry, having eaten nothing all day. You select the best restaurant in your city and ask the waiter for the finest steak on his menu. He replies that the filet mignon is the house favorite, and you order it charcoal-broiled, medium rare. The waiter returns twenty minutes later with the fare and sets it before you. There in the center of a large plate is a lonely piece of meat, one inch square, flanked by a single bit of potato.

You complain vigorously to the waiter, "Is this what you call a steak dinner?"

He then replies, "Sir, how can you criticize us before you taste that meat? I have brought you one square inch of the finest steak money can buy. It is cooked to perfection, salted with care, and served while hot. In fact, I doubt if you could get a better piece of meat anywhere in the city. I'll admit that the serving is small, but after all, sir, everyone knows that it isn't the quantity that matters; it's the quality that counts in steak dinners."

"Nonsense!" you reply, and I certainly agree. You see, the subtlety of this simple phrase is that it puts two necessary virtues in opposition to one another and invites us to choose between them. If quantity and quality are worthwhile ingredients in family relationships, then why not give our kids *both?* It is insufficient to toss our "hungry" children an occasional bite of steak, even if it is prime, corn-fed filet mignon.

Without meaning any disrespect to you for asking this question, my concern is that the quantity-versus-quality cliche has become, perhaps, a rationalization for giving our kids *neither!* This phrase has been bandied about by over-committed and harassed parents who feel guilty about the lack of time they spend with their children. Their boys and girls are parked at child care centers during the day and with baby-sitters at night, leaving little time for traditional parenting activities. And to handle the discomfort of neglecting their children, Mom and Dad cling to a catch phrase that makes it seem so healthy and proper: "Well, you know, it's not the *quantity* of time that matters, it's the *quality* of your togetherness that counts." I maintain that this convenient generalization simply won't hold water.[10]

If it were possible to put a speedometer on a particular style of living, our family would consistently break the sound barrier. We're all so incredibly busy that we hardly have any home life at all. What effect does this breathless pace have on a family, and especially on kids?
The inevitable loser from this life in the fast lane is the little guy who is leaning against the wall with his hands in the pockets of his blue jeans. He misses his father during the long days and tags around after him at night, saying, "Play ball, Dad!" But Dad is pooped. Besides, he has a briefcase full of work to be done. Mom had promised to take him to the park this afternoon, but then she had to go to that Women's Auxiliary meeting at the last minute. The lad gets the message—his folks are busy again. So he drifts into the family room and watches two hours of pointless cartoons and reruns on television.

Children just don't fit into a "to do" list very well. It takes time to be an effective parent when children are small. It takes time to introduce them to good books—it takes time to fly kites and play punch ball and put together jigsaw puzzles. It takes time to listen, once more, to the skinned-knee episode and talk about the bird with the broken wing. These are the building blocks of esteem, held together with the mortar of love. But they seldom materialize amidst busy timetables. Instead, crowded lives produce fatigue—and fatigue produces irritability—and irritability produces indifference—and indifference can be interpreted by the child as a lack of genuine affection and personal esteem.

As the commercial says, "Slow down, America!" What is your rush, anyway? Don't you know your children will be gone so quickly and you will have nothing but blurred memories of those years when they needed you? I'm not suggesting that we invest our entire adult lives into the next generation, nor must everyone become parents. But once those children are here, they had better fit into our schedule somewhere.[11]

My family lives together under one roof and we share the same last name. But we don't "feel" like a family. We're so rushed and stressed by the routine pressures of living that I sometimes feel I hardly know my wife and kids. How can I begin to put a sense of togetherness into this harried household? How do *you* put meaningful activities into your family?

I've written and spoken extensively on the dangers of overcommitment and "routine panic," and I will not repeat that warning here, except to say that you should make a concerted effort to slow the pace at which your family is running. Beyond that advice, however, I would emphasize the importance of creating special *traditions* in your home. By traditions I'm referring to those recurring events and behaviors that are anticipated, especially by children, as times of closeness and fellowship between loved ones.

For example, one of the most important holiday traditions in our family centers around food. Each year during Thanksgiving and Christmas, the women prepare tremendous meals, involving the traditional holiday menu of turkey and all that goes with it. A great favorite is a fruit dish called ambrosia, containing sectioned oranges and peeled grapes. The family peels the grapes together the night before Thanksgiving.

The Thanksgiving and Christmas holidays are wonderful experiences for all of us. There's laughter and warm family interaction through the day. We look forward to that festive season, not just for the food, but for what happens between loved ones who convene.

We not only attempt to serve traditional Thanksgiving and Christmas meals, but we try to have specific foods on each holiday throughout the year. On New Year's Day, for reasons which I cannot explain, we enjoy a southern meal of pinto beans cooked at least eight hours with large chunks of lean ham, served with cornbread and little onions. It's so good! On July 4th we invite thirty or more friends and serve barbecued hamburgers and baked beans in the backyard. This has become a prelude to the fireworks display.

Obviously, many of our traditions (but not all) focus on the enjoyable activity of eating together. Another example occurs immediately *prior* to the Thanksgiving dinner. After the food is on the table and family members are seated, I read a passage of Scripture and Shirley tells the story of the Pilgrims who thanked God for helping them survive the ravages of winter. Then each person is given two kernels of Indian corn to symbolize the blessings he or she is most thankful for that year. A basket is passed and every member drops in the corn while sharing their two richest blessings from God during that year. Our expressions of thankfulness inevitably involve people—children and grandparents and other loved ones. As the basket moves around the table, tears of appreciation and love are evident on many faces. It is one of the most beautiful moments of the year.

This brings me back to the question about harried homes. The great value of traditions is that they give a family a sense of identity and belonging. All of us desperately need to feel that we're not just part of a busy cluster of people living together in a house, but we're a living, breathing family that's conscious of our uniqueness, our character, and our heritage. That feeling is the only antidote for the loneliness and isolation that characterize so many homes today.

I know that for the sake of my marriage and my family I should not overcommit myself. But what do I do with the guilt feelings I have when I neglect worthwhile things, especially with regard to my duties in the church?
I think God wants us to exercise common sense in the assignments we accept—even those involving worthwhile

causes. Inevitably, this judgment will require us to decline some responsibilities in order to maintain a balance between work, recreation, family activities, exercise, devotions, etc. If too many good activities are attempted, other good objectives will be sacrificed. That is like installing a new sprinkler system in a yard and putting too many outlets on the line. When that occurs, *nothing* is watered properly.

I'm reminded, also, of a magazine advertisement that explained how Gallo Wines are produced. It contained a message that is relevant to this discussion. I had not previously known that grape farmers not only prune dead branches from their vines, but they also eliminate a certain amount of the fruit-producing branches. In other words, they sacrifice some of the crop so that what fruit is left will be better. Do you see the relevance to our lives today?

Notice these Bible verses from John 15:1, 2:

> I am the true Vine, and my Father is the Gardener. He lops off every branch that doesn't produce and he prunes those branches that bear fruit for even larger crops.

It is necessary in the Christian life to eliminate some good things from your schedule so that the other things you do are done better. That is the best way to achieve better quality in the good activities that remain. But let me add a warning that this objective can easily become a rationalization for carrying no responsibility in the church or bearing no burden for the needs of others. That is certainly not a justifiable position to take.[12]

We are not able financially to take long car trips or get into expensive hobbies, like skiing. Could you suggest some simple traditions that will appeal to small children?
You don't have to spend a lot of money to preserve meaningful family life. Children love daily routine activities of the simplest kind. They enjoy hearing the same stories a thousand times over, and they'll laugh at the same jokes until you're ready to climb the wall from repeating them. You can turn the routine chores of living into times of warmth and closeness if you give a little thought to them. The key is *repetition*, which conveys the feeling of tradition.

Let me give an example. When my family was younger I attempted as often as possible to put the children to bed in the evening. By that time of night, my wife was exhausted and she appreciated the help. It also guaranteed me at least fifteen to twenty minutes with the kids no matter how busy I had been that day.

The responsibility included diapering Ryan during the first three years of his life. (It took him a while to overcome that requirement, as it does with all children.) I figured if I had to put a diaper on a squirming toddler, I might as well turn the activity into something that would be fun for both of us. So we played a little game each night. I would talk to the pins as I was diapering my son. I would say, "Pins, don't stick him; I don't really think you ought to stick him. See, he's being still; he's not wiggling around. Tonight you don't have to stick him; maybe tomorrow night, but don't stick him tonight." Ryan loved the game! He'd listen quietly, his eyes as big as half dollars. If he wiggled too much and kept me from getting his diapers on, I would scrape the point of the pin gently on his leg, not enough to hurt, but enough to make him aware of it. He'd look up at me and say, "Those mean ol' pins sticked me, Daddy!" We would both grin. And every night Ryan would say without fail, "Talk to the pins, Daddy!" It was something we did together, turning a routine activity into something of pleasure between a father and his toddler.

I'm reminded of what Howard Hendricks said when his children were grown. He asked them what they most enjoyed about their childhood—the vacations they had taken, the parks they had visited, and all the moments that they had enjoyed together. Their answer surprised him. What they appreciated most were the times when he had gotten down on the floor and fought with them!

My daughter felt the same way when she was young. She would rather fight with me than go to Disneyland or the zoo! After we had had a tussle that left me exhausted, she always thanked me for fighting with her. For some reason, kids love that wild activity. (Mothers hate it.) There's a kind of informal love that transpires in a playful romp that doesn't occur any other way.

I also like the idea of reserving one night a week for oral reading with the family. Sometimes that's difficult to accomplish with children of varying ages, but if your sons and daughters are clustered in age, I think it's a great activity. You can read *Tom Sawyer* and other books that have been so popular down through the ages. The idea is to read *together* as a family.

In short, I believe many Americans have forgotten the value of characteristics and activities which identify the families as unique and different. This benefit was beautifully illustrated by the stage play *Fiddler on the Roof.* What gave the violinist his stability and balance on his precarious perch? It was *tradition*—which told every person who he was. I want to give that same heritage to my children.[13]

Can these traditions be useful in teaching spiritual values as well?

They certainly can. In fact, by far the most *important* traditions are those that help instill Christian principles and elements of the Judeo-Christian heritage in our children. This gives a boy or girl an additional sense of history and of his/her place in it. If you asked me to indicate *who I am* today, my answer would reflect the Christian values and teachings that I learned as a child. Those understandings began even before I could talk.

Thus, a vital fringe benefit of Christianity is the tremendous sense of identity that grows out of knowing Jesus Christ. Each child can be made aware, beyond a shadow of doubt, that he is a personal creation of God. He can know that the Creator has a plan for his life and that Jesus died for him. I'm convinced that there is no greater sense of self-esteem and personal worth than the personal awareness that comes from deeply ingrained spiritual values. This understanding answers the important questions of life, including "Who am I?" "Who loves me?" "Where am I going?" and "What is the purpose of life?" Only Christ can provide the answers to these questions which give meaning to this earthly experience.

What would you do if your eighteen-year-old son decided to become a social dropout and run away from home?

It is difficult for anyone to know exactly how he would face a given crisis, but I can tell you what I think would be the best reaction under those circumstances. Without nagging and whining, I would hope to influence the boy to change his mind before he made a mistake. If he could not be dissuaded, I would have to let him go. It is not wise for parents to be too demanding and authoritative with an older teenager; they may force him to defy their authority just to prove his independence and adulthood. Besides this, if they pound on the table, wring their hands, and scream at their wayward son, he will not feel the full responsibility for his own behavior. When Mom and Dad are too emotionally involved with him, he can expect them to bail him out if he runs into trouble. I think it is much wiser to treat the late adolescent like an adult; he's more likely to act like one if he is given the status offered to other adults. The appropriate parental reaction should be: "John, you know I feel you are making a choice that will haunt you for many years. I want you to sit down with me and we will analyze the pros and cons; then the final decision will be yours. I will not stand in your way." John knows that the responsibility is on his shoulders. Beginning in middle adolescence, parents should give a child more and more responsibility each year, so that when he gets beyond their control he will no longer need it.

The Gospel of St. Luke contains an amazingly relevant story of a young dropout. It is commonly known as the parable of the prodigal son. Read the story in Luke 15 and then note that it contains several important messages that are highly relevant to our day. First, the father did not try to locate his son and drag him home. The boy was apparently old enough to make his own decision and the father allowed him the privilege of determining his course.

Second, the father did not come to his rescue during the financial stress that followed. He didn't send money. There were no well-meaning church groups that helped support his folly. Note in verses 16 and 17, "No one gave him anything . . . he finally came to his senses" (TLB). Perhaps we sometimes keep our children from coming to their senses by preventing them from feeling the consequences of their own mistakes. When a teenager gets a speeding citation, *he* should pay for it. When he wrecks his car, *he* should have it fixed. When he gets suspended from school, *he* should take the consequences without parental protests to the school. He will learn from these adversities. The parent who is too quick to bail his child out of difficulty may be doing him a disservice.

Third, the father welcomed his son home without belittling him or demanding reparations. He didn't say, "I told you you'd make a mess of things!" or "You've embarrassed your mom and me to death. Everyone is talking about what a terrible son we've raised!" Instead, he revealed the depth of his love by saying, "He was lost and is found!"[14]

I want to ask you a very personal question. Your books deal with practical aspects of everyday living. They offer solutions and suggestions for handling the typical frustrations and problems of parenthood and marriage. But that makes me wonder about your own family. Does your home always run smoothly? Do you ever feel like a failure as a father? And if so, how do you deal with self-doubt and recrimination?

I have been asked this question many times, although the answer should surprise no one. Shirley and I experience the same frustrations and pressures that others face. Our behavior is not always exemplary, nor is that of our children. And our household can become very hectic at times.

Perhaps I can best illustrate my reply by describing the day we now refer to as "Black Sunday." For some reason, the Sabbath can be the most frustrating day of the week for us, especially during the morning hours. I've found that other parents also experience tensions during the "get 'em ready for church" routine. But Black Sunday was especially chaotic. We began that day by getting up too late, meaning everyone had to rush to get to church on time. That produced emotional pressure, especially for Shirley and me. Then there was the matter of the spilt milk at breakfast and the black shoe polish on the floor. And, of course, Ryan got dressed first, enabling him to slip out the back door and get himself dirty from head to toe. It was necessary to take him down to the skin and start over with clean clothes once more. Instead of handling these irritants as they arose, we began criticizing one another and hurling accusations back and forth. At least one spanking was delivered, as I recall, and another three or four were promised. Yes, it was a day to be remembered (or forgotten). Finally, four harried people managed to stumble into church, ready for a great spiritual blessing, no doubt. There's no pastor in the world who could have moved us on that morning.

I felt guilty throughout the day for the strident tone of our home on that Black Sunday. Sure, our children shared the blame, but they were merely responding to our disorganization. Shirley and I had overslept, and that's where the conflict originated.

After the evening service, I called the family together around the kitchen table. I began by describing the kind of day we had had, and asked each person to forgive me for my part in it. Furthermore, I said that I thought we should give each member of the family an opportunity to say whatever he or she was feeling inside.

Ryan was given the first shot, and he fired it at his mother. "You've been a real grouch today, Mom!" he said with feeling. "You've blamed me for everything I've done all day long."

Danae then poured out her hostilities and frustrations. Finally, Shirley and I had an opportunity to explain the tensions that had caused our overreaction.

It was a valuable time of ventilation and honesty that drew us together once more. We then had prayer as a family and asked the Lord to help us live and work together in love and harmony.

My point is that *every* family has moments when they violate all the rules—even departing from the Christian principles by which they have lived. Fatigue itself can damage all the high ideals which have been recommended to parents in seminars and books and sermons. The important question is, how do mothers and fathers reestablish friendship within their families when the storm has passed? Open, nonthreatening discussion offers one solution to that situation.

Returning to the question, let's acknowledge that a psychologist can no more prevent all emotional distress for his family than a physician can circumvent disease in his. We live in an imperfect world which inflicts struggles on us all. Nevertheless, biblical principles offer the most healthy approach to family living—even turning stress to our advantage. (Someday I'll tell you about Black Monday.)[15]

Our financial problems are getting more frustrating every day. Do you have any suggestions?
There are thousands of books available for those who want to gain control of their monetary resources, and I am no authority on that subject. Thus, my comments on this topic will be brief and to the point. My one contribution is in opposition to the lust for more and more things—leading us to buy that which we neither need nor can afford.

Though I can make no claim to wealth, I have tasted most of the things Americans hunger for: new cars, an attractive home, and gadgets and devices which promise to set us free. Looking at those materialistic possessions from the other side of the cash register, I can tell you that they don't deliver the satisfaction they advertise! On the contrary, I have found great wisdom in the adage, "That which you own will eventually own you!" How true that is. Having surrendered my hard-earned dollars for a new object only obligates me to maintain and protect it; instead of its contributing to my pleasure, I must spend my precious Saturdays oiling it, mowing it, painting it, repairing it, cleaning it, or calling the Salvation Army to haul it off. The time I might have invested in worthwhile family activities is spent in slavery to a depreciating piece of junk.

Let me ask you to recall *the* most worthless, unnecessary expenditure you have made in the last year. Perhaps it was an electric can opener which now sits in the garage, or a suit of clothes which will never be worn. Do you realize that this item was not purchased with your money; it was bought with your time which you traded for money? In effect, you swapped a certain proportion of your alloted days on earth for that piece of junk which now clutters your home. Furthermore, no power on earth could retrieve the time which you squandered on its purchase. It is gone forever. We are investing our lives in worthless materialism, both in the original expenditures and on subsequent upkeep and maintenance.

Do I sound a bit preachy in this discourse? Perhaps it is because I am condemning my own way of life. I am sick of the tyranny of things! But I'm also addressing the "have nots," those multitudes who are depressed because they own so little. How many women today are depressed because they lack something which either wasn't invented or wasn't fashionable fifty years ago? How many families are discontented with their two-bedroom house, when it would have been considered entirely adequate in the 1800s? How many men will have heart attacks this year from striving to achieve an ever-increasing salary? How many families will court financial ruin just to keep up with the Joneses, and then find to their dismay that the Joneses have refinanced and are ahead again?

The utter folly of materialism was dramatically emphasized during my most recent trip to England. As I toured the museums and historical buildings, I was struck by what I called "empty castles." Standing there in the lonely fog were the edifices constructed by proud men who thought they owned them. But where are those men today? All are gone and most are forgotten. The hollow castles they left behind stand as monuments to the physical vulnerability and impermanence of the men who built them. Not one has survived to claim his possession. As Jesus said of the rich fool who was about to die and leave his wealth, "Then whose shall those things be, which thou hast provided?" (Luke 12:20 KJV)

May I say with the strongest conviction that I want to leave more than "empty castles" behind me when I die. At forty-five years of age, I realize how rapidly my life is passing before my eyes. Time is like a well-greased string which slides through my taut fingers. I've tried vainly to hold it or even slow its pace, but it only accelerates year by year. Just as surely as the past twenty years evaporated so quickly, the next three or four decades will soon be gone. So there is no better time than now for me (and you) to assess the values which are worthy of my time and effort. Having made that evaluation, I have concluded that the accumulation of wealth, even if I could achieve it, is an insufficient reason for living. When I reach the end of my days, a moment or two from now, I must look backward on something more meaningful than the pursuit of houses and land and machines and stocks and bonds. Nor is fame of any lasting benefit. I will consider my earthly existence to have been wasted unless I can recall a loving family, a consistent investment in the lives of people, and an earnest attempt to serve the God who made me. Nothing else makes much sense, and certainly nothing else is worthy of my agitation! How about you?[16]

Considering how difficult it is to be good parents, why should anyone want to have children? Is it worth it?

Parenthood is costly and complex, no doubt about that. I'm reminded of a woman with seven rambunctious children who boarded a Los Angeles bus and sat in the seat behind me. Her hair was a mess and the black circles under her eyes revealed a state of utter exhaustion. As she stumbled past me with her wiggling tribe, I asked, "Do all those children belong to you, or is this some kind of picnic?"

She looked at me through squinted eyes and said, "They're all mine, and believe me, it's no picnic!"

The woman is right. Parenthood is no job for sissies. Am I suggesting, then, that newly married couples should remain childless? Certainly not! The family that loves children and wants to experience the thrill of procreation should not be frightened by the challenge of parenthood. Speaking from my own perspective as a father, there has been no greater moment in my life than when I gazed into the eyes of my infant daughter, and five years later, my son. What could be more exciting than seeing those tiny human beings begin to blossom and grow and learn and love? And what reward could be more meaningful than having my little boy or girl climb onto my lap as I sit by the fire, hug my neck, and whisper, "I love you, Dad."

Oh, yes, children are expensive, but they're worth the price. Besides, nothing worth having comes cheap.[17]

SECTION 2
SPIRITUAL TRAINING OF CHILDREN

Should a child be allowed to "decide for himself" on matters related to his concept of God? Aren't we forcing our religion down his throat when we tell him what he must believe?

Let me answer that question with an illustration from nature. A little gosling (baby goose) has a peculiar characteristic that is relevant at this point. Shortly after he hatches from his shell he will become attached, or "imprinted," to the first thing that he sees moving near him. From that time forward, he will follow that particular object when it moves in his vicinity. Ordinarily, he becomes imprinted to the mother goose who was on hand to hatch the new generation. If she is removed, however, the gosling will settle for any mobile substitute, whether alive or not. In fact, a gosling will become most easily attached to a blue football bladder, dragged by on a string. A week later, he'll fall in line behind the bladder as it scoots by him. Time is the critical factor in this process. The gosling is vulnerable to imprinting for only a few seconds after he hatches from the shell; if that opportunity is lost, it cannot be regained later. In other words, there is a critical, brief period in the life of a gosling when this instinctual learning is possible.

There is also a critical period when certain kinds of instruction are possible in the life of the child. Although humans have no instincts (only drives, reflexes, urges, etc.), there is a brief period during childhood when youngsters are vulnerable to religious training. Their concepts of right and wrong, which Freud called the superego, are formulated during this time, and their view of God begins to solidify. As in the case of the gosling, the opportunity of that period must be seized when it is available. Leaders of the Catholic Church have been widely quoted as saying, "Give us a child until he is seven years old and we'll have him for life"; their affirmation is usually correct, because permanent attitudes can be instilled during these seven vulnerable years. Unfortunately, however, the opposite is also true. The absence or misapplication of instruction through that prime-time period may place a severe limitation on the depth of the child's later devotion to God. When parents say they are going to withhold indoctrination from their small child, allowing him to "decide for himself," they are almost guaranteeing that he will "decide" in the negative. If a parent wants his child to have a meaningful faith, he must give up any misguided attempts at objectivity. The child listens closely to discover just how much his parent believes what he is preaching; any indecision or ethical confusion from the parent is likely to be magnified in the child.[1]

My wife and I have bedtime prayer with our child each night, and he goes to Sunday school and church every week. Still, I don't feel that this is enough to ensure his religious development. What more can I do to foster his spiritual growth at this time when his attention span is so limited?

The answer was provided by Moses as he wrote more than 4,000 years ago in the book of Deuteronomy: "You must teach them [the principles and commandments of God] to your children and talk about them when you are at home or out for a walk; at bedtime and the first thing in the morning. Tie them to your finger, wear them on your forehead, and write them on the doorposts of your house!" (Deut. 6:7-9 TLB). In other words, we can't instill these attitudes during a brief bedtime prayer, or during formalized training sessions. We must *live* them from morning to night. They should be reinforced during our casual conversation, being punctuated with illustrations, demonstrations, compliments, and chastisement. This teaching task is, I believe, *the* most important assignment God has given to us as parents.[2]

It is difficult for us to have meaningful devotions as a family because our young children seem so bored and uninvolved. They yawn and squirm and giggle while we

are reading from the Bible. On the other hand, we feel it is important to teach them to pray and study God's Word. Can you help us deal with this dilemma?

The one key word to family devotions is *brevity*. Children can't be expected to comprehend and appreciate lengthy adult spiritual activities. Four or five minutes devoted to one or two Bible verses, followed by a short prayer, usually represents the limits of attention during the preschool years. To force young children to comprehend eternal truths in an eternal devotional can be eternally dangerous.[3]

How is the concept of God established in the mind of the child?

It is a well-known fact that a child identifies his parents with God, whether or not the adults want that role. While yielding to their loving leadership, for example, children are also learning to yield to the benevolent leadership of God Himself.

We have the responsibility of reflecting the two aspects of divine nature to the next generation. First, our Heavenly Father is a God of unlimited love, and our children must become acquainted with His mercy and tenderness through our own love toward them. But make no mistake about it, our Lord is also the possessor of majestic authority! The universe is ordered by a supreme Lord who requires obedience from His children and has warned them that "the wages of sin is death." To show our little ones love without authority is as serious a distortion of God's nature as to reveal an iron-fisted authority without love.[4]

What is the most critical period in the spiritual training of young children?

I believe the fifth year of a child's life is the most critical. Up to that time, he believes in God because his parents tell him it is the thing to do. At about five or six years of age he comes to a fork in the road: either he begins to reach out and accept the concept as his own, or he does not. At that point, he may "buy it" and put his feet down onto a more solid foundation—or he may start to doubt it, laying the basis for rejection.

I certainly don't mean to imply that parents should wait until the child is five or six to begin spiritual training. Nor are subsequent years unimportant. But I am convinced that our most diligent efforts in the home, and our best teachers in

Sunday school, ought to be applied to the child of five or six years. There are crucial crossroads after that, but this is the first important one.[5]

Many people believe that children are basically "good," and only learn to do wrong from their parents and culture. Do you agree?

If they mean that all children are worthy and deserving of our love and respect, I certainly do agree. But if they believe that children are by nature unselfish, giving, and sinless before God, I must disagree. I wish that assessment of human nature were accurate, but it contradicts scriptural understandings. Jeremiah wrote: "The heart is deceitful above all things, and desperately wicked: who can know it?" (Jer. 17:9 KJV). Jeremiah's inspired insight into human nature is validated by the sordid history of mankind. The path of civilization is blotted by murder, war, rape, and plundering from the time of Adam forward. This record of evil makes it difficult to hold to the pollyannish view that children are pure and holy at birth and merely learn to do wrong from their misguided parents. Surely during the past 6,000 years, there must have been at least *one* generation for whom parents did things right. Yet greed, lust, and selfishness have characterized us all. Is this nature also evident in children? King David thought so, for he confessed, ". . . in sin did my mother conceive me" (Psa. 51:5 KJV).

What meaningful difference, then, is made by the distinction between the two views of children? Practically everything, in fact. Parents who believe all toddlers are infused with goodness and sunshine are urged to get out of the way and let their pleasant nature unfold. On the other hand, parents who recognize the inevitable internal war between good and evil will do their best to influence the child's choices—to shape his will and provide a solid spiritual foundation. They acknowledge the dangers of adult defiance as expressed in 1 Samuel 15:23—"For rebellion is as bad as the sin of witchcraft, and stubbornness is as bad as worshiping idols" (TLB).[6]

Parents have been commanded in the Bible to "train up a child in the way he should go." But this poses a critical question: What way should he go? If the first seven years

represent the "prime time" for religious training, what should be taught during this period? What experiences should be included? What values should be emphasized? You've asked an excellent question. It is my strong belief that a child should be exposed to a carefully conceived, systematic program of religious training. Yet we are much too haphazard about this matter. Perhaps we would hit the mark more often if we more clearly recognized the precise target.

Listed below is a "Checklist for Spiritual Training"—a set of targets at which to aim. Many of the items require maturity which children lack, and we should not try to make adult Christians out of our immature youngsters. But we can gently urge them toward these goals—these targets—during the impressionable years of childhood.

Essentially, the five scriptural concepts which follow should be consciously taught, providing the foundation on which all future doctrine and faith will rest. I encourage every Christian parent to evaluate his child's understanding of these five areas:

CONCEPT I: "And thou shalt love the Lord thy God with all thy heart" (Mark 12:30 KJV).

1. Is your child learning of the love of God through the love, tenderness, and mercy of his parents? (most important)
2. Is he learning to talk about the Lord, and to include Him in his thoughts and plans?
3. Is he learning to turn to Jesus for help whenever he is frightened or anxious or lonely?
4. Is he learning to read the Bible?
5. Is he learning to pray?
6. Is he learning the meaning of faith and trust?
7. Is he learning the joy of the Christian way of life?
8. Is he learning the beauty of Jesus' birth and death?

CONCEPT II: "Thou shalt love thy neighbor as thyself" (Mark 12:31 KJV).

1. Is he learning to understand and empathize with the feelings of others?
2. Is he learning not to be selfish and demanding?
3. Is he learning to share?
4. Is he learning not to gossip and criticize others?
5. Is he learning to accept himself?

CONCEPT III: "Teach me to do thy will; for thou art my God" (Psa. 143:10 KJV).

1. Is he learning to obey his parents as preparation for later obedience to God? (most important)
2. Is he learning to behave properly in church—God's house?
3. Is he learning a healthy appreciation for both aspects of God's nature: love and justice?
4. Is he learning that there are many forms of benevolent authority outside himself to which he must submit?
5. Is he learning the meaning of sin and its inevitable consequences?

CONCEPT IV: "Fear God, and keep his commandments: for this is the whole duty of man" (Eccles. 12:13 KJV).
1. Is he learning to be truthful and honest?
2. Is he learning to keep the Sabbath day holy?
3. Is he learning the relative insignificance of materialism?
4. Is he learning the meaning of the Christian family, and the faithfulness to it which God intends?
5. Is he learning to follow the dictates of his own conscience?

CONCEPT V: "But the fruit of the Spirit is . . . self-control" (Gal. 5:22, 23 RSV).
1. Is he learning to give a portion of his allowance (and other money) to God?
2. Is he learning to control his impulses?
3. Is he learning to work and carry responsibility?
4. Is he learning the vast difference between self-worth and egotistical pride?
5. Is he learning to bow in reverence before the God of the universe?

In summary, your child's first seven years should prepare him to say, at the age of accountability, "Here I am, Lord, send me!"[7]

My four-year-old frequently comes running home in tears because she has been hit by one of her little friends. I have taught her that it is not right to hit others, but now they are making life miserable for my little girl. As a Christian parent, what should I tell her about defending herself?

You were wise to teach your daughter not to hit and hurt others, but self-defense is another matter. Children can be unmerciful in their torment of a defenseless child. When youngsters play together, they each want to have the best toys and determine the ground rules to their own advantage. If they find they can predominate by simply flinging a well-aimed fist at the nose of their playmate, someone is likely to get hurt. I'm sure there are Christians who disagree with me on this issue, but I believe you should teach your child to defend herself when attacked. Later, she can be taught to "turn the other cheek," which even mature adults find difficult to implement.

I recently consulted with a mother who was worried about her small daughter's inability to protect herself from aggression. There was one child in their neighborhood who would crack three-year-old Ann in the face at the slightest provocation. This little bully, named Joan, was very small and feminine, but she never felt the sting of retaliation because Ann had been taught not to fight back. I recommended that Ann's mother tell her to return Joan's attack if Joan hits first. Several days later the mother heard a loud altercation outside, followed by a brief scuffle. Then Joan began crying and went home. Ann walked casually into the house with her hands in her pockets, and explained, "Joan socked me so I had to help her remember not to hit me again." Ann had efficiently returned an eye for an eye and a tooth for a tooth. She and Joan have played together much more peacefully since that time.

Generally speaking, a parent should emphasize the foolishness of fighting. But to force a child to stand passively while being clobbered is to leave him at the mercy of his cold-blooded peers.[8]

Do you think children between five and ten should be allowed to listen to rock music on the radio?
No. Rock music is an expression of an adolescent culture. The words of teenagers' songs deal with dating, broken hearts, drug usage and luv-luv-luv. This is just what you don't want your seven-year-old thinking about. Instead, his world of excitement should consist of adventure books, Disney-type productions, and family activities—camping, fishing, sporting events, games, etc.

On the other hand, it is unwise to appear dictatorial and oppressive in such matters. I would suggest that you keep your preteen so involved with wholesome activities that he does not need to dream of the days to come.[9]

How can I help my child develop wholesome, accepting attitudes toward people of other racial and ethnic groups?

There is no substitute for parental modeling of the attitudes we wish to teach. Someone wrote, "The footsteps a child follows are most likely to be the ones his parents thought they covered up." It is true. Our children are watching us carefully, and they instinctively imitate our behavior. Therefore, we can hardly expect them to be kind to all of God's children if we are prejudiced and rejecting. Likewise, we will be unable to teach appreciativeness if we never say, "please" or "thank you" at home or abroad. We will not produce honest children if we teach them to lie to the bill collector on the phone by saying, "Dad's not home." In these matters, our boys and girls instantly discern the gap between what we say and what we do. And of the two choices, they usually identify with our behavior and ignore our empty proclamations.[10]

I'm trying to raise and train two boys without the help of a husband and father, and I'm not handling the assignment very well. Shouldn't the church be doing something to help me as a single parent?

Yes, it is clearly the task of the church to assist you with your parenting responsibilities. This requirement is implicit in Jesus' commandment that we love and support the needy in all walks of life. He said, "Inasmuch as ye have done it unto the least of these, my brethren, ye have done it unto me." If Jesus meant these words, and He obviously did, then our effort on behalf of a fatherless or motherless child is seen by the Creator of the universe as a direct service to Himself!

But the commandment to Christians is more explicitly stated in James 1:27: "The Christian who is pure and without fault, from God the Father's point of view, is the one who takes care of orphans and widows, and who remains true to the Lord" (TLB).

These Scriptures make it clear that we Christians are going to be held accountable for how well we reach out to those in need. The men of the church should take fatherless boys to the park, showing them how to throw a ball or catch a Frisbee. They should look for opportunities to reshingle or repaint a single mother's house, or do those repair jobs that she would find difficult to do even if she were not carrying heavy work responsibilities. And she might be in need of cash when her

children are small. The biblical assignment is clear: wherever
the need exists, it should be met by Christian men of the
church![11]

**My husband and I are missionaries and have recently
been assigned to a remote area of Colombia. Our ministry
will be with an Indian culture which can only be reached
by horseback or on foot. My concern is for our children,
ages seven and nine, and their educational future. There
are no schools near our new location, of course, and the
nearest boarding facility will be more than 200 miles
away. Because of the cost of travel, we would only be able
to see them through the summers and perhaps at one
other time during the year. Although I could teach them
the academic subjects required between now and high
school years, they obviously need social contact with
their peers and we don't want to deprive them of those
experiences. Would you recommend keeping them with
us, or sending them away to school?**

"What will we do with the children?" That is often the most
difficult question missionaries must answer. I don't propose to
have final solutions to this thorny problem, although I do have
some definite views on the subject. I've dealt with the children
of missionaries, many of whom had become bitter and resentful
of the sacrifices they were required to make. They were
deprived of a secure home at a critical stage in their
development and experienced deep emotional wounds in the
process. Consequently, adolescent rebellion was common
among these angry young people who resented their parents
and the God who sent them abroad.

Based on these observations, it is my firm conviction that the
family unit of missionaries should remain intact, if at all
possible. I cannot overemphasize the importance of parental
support and love during the formative years of life. A child's
sense of security and well-being is primarily rooted in the
stability of his home and family. Therefore, he is certain to be
shaken by separation not only from his parents, but also from
his friends and the familiar surroundings of his own culture. He
suddenly finds himself in a lonely dormitory in a foreign land
where he may face rejection and pressures that threaten to
overwhelm him. I can think of no better method of producing
emotional (and spiritual) problems in a vulnerable child!

My friend Dr. Paul Cunningham expressed a similar view during a conference on family life. His comments were recorded by a court reporter and are quoted below, with Dr. Cunningham's permission:

> I am married to a missionary's daughter who at the age of five and a half was sent to boarding school in Africa, where she saw her parents about three times a year. This represents the most severe kind of sacrifice that a missionary has to face. I have had the privilege of ministering to the children of missionaries, and I think it can be safely said, and I want to say this very carefully, that those children who have had this experience often never fully recover from it.
>
> My wife, for example, was "put down" when she was in the school because of the strong anti-American sentiment there. She was the only American in her school. We're not talking about a child of ten or twelve years old, but only six. All in all, it has made her a tremendously strong person, and I doubt if she would have been all that she is to me and to our children had she not had those tough experiences. But at the same time, were she not from strong English stock with tremendous gifts and graces, I don't know . . . maybe she would not have survived, because others haven't.
>
> I can't feel that this is a good policy at this point to make this the only answer for these families . . . to separate tender little children from their parents. I know of one situation, for example, where the children have to take a long ride in a riverboat to see their parents; I'm talking about little children. It's a trip of several hours to their mission compound. Their mother says goodbye to them in the fall, and she does not see them for many months because of the expense of traveling. They could be taken by helicopter instead of the riverboat ride, but they don't have the money. We must do something to assist people like this, whatever the cost.

Dr. Cunningham and I agree that the true issue may actually be one of priorities. Meaningful family involvement outranks educational considerations by a wide margin, in my view. Furthermore, contact with parents during the early years is even more important than contact with peers. And finally, even missionaries (who have been called to a life of sacrifice and service) must reserve some of their resources for their own families. After all, a lifetime of successes on a foreign field will be rather pale and insignificant to those who lose their own children.[12]

My wife and I disagree strongly about the role of materialism in the lives of our kids. She feels that we should give them the toys and games that we never had as kids. At Christmas time, we stack gifts knee-deep around the tree, and then spend the next six months trying to pay for all the stuff we have bought. And, of course, the grandparents lavish gifts on our children throughout the year. I feel this is a mistake, even if we could afford to do what we are doing. What is your view on materialism in the life of a child?

I also have concerns about giving kids too many things, which often reflects our inability to say "no" to them. During the hardships of the Great Depression, it was very simple for parents to tell their children that they couldn't afford to buy them everything they wanted; Dad could barely keep bread on the table. But in opulent times, the parental task becomes more difficult. It takes considerably more courage to say, "No, I won't buy you Baby-Blow-Her-Nose," than it did to say, "I'm sorry, but you know we can't afford to buy that doll." The child's lust for expensive toys is carefully generated through millions of dollars spent on TV advertising by toy manufacturers. Their commercials are skillfully made so that the toys look like full-sized copies of their real counterparts: jet airplanes, robot monsters, and automatic rifles. The little buyer sits open-mouthed in utter fascination. Five minutes later he begins a campaign that will eventually cost his dad $14.95 plus batteries and tax. The trouble is, Dad probably *can* afford to buy the new item, if not with cash, at least with his magic credit card. And when three other children on the block get the coveted toys, Mom and Dad begin to feel the pressure, and even the guilt. They feel selfish because they have indulged themselves for similar luxuries. Suppose the parents are courageous enough to resist the child's urging; he is not blocked—grandparents are notoriously easy to "con." Even if the child is unsuccessful in getting his parents or grandparents to buy what he wants, there is an annual foolproof resource: Santa Claus! When Junior asks Santa to bring him something, his parents are in an inescapable trap. What can they say, "Santa can't afford it"? Is Santa going to forget and disappoint him? No, the toy will be on Santa's sleigh.

Some would ask, "And why not? Why shouldn't we let our children enjoy the fruits of our good times?" Certainly I would not deny the child a reasonable quantity of the things he craves. But many American children are inundated with excesses that work toward their detriment. It has been said that prosperity offers a greater test of character than does adversity, and I'm inclined to agree. There are few conditions that inhibit a sense of appreciation more than for a child to feel he is entitled to whatever he wants, whenever he wants it. It is enlightening to watch as a child tears open stacks of presents at his birthday party or perhaps at Christmas time. One after another, the expensive contents are tossed aside with little more than a glance. The child's mother is made uneasy by this lack of enthusiasm and appreciation, so she says, "Oh, Marvin! Look what it is! It's a little tape recorder! What do you say to Grandmother? Give Grandmother a big hug. Did you hear me, Marvin? Go give Grams a big hug and kiss." Marvin may or may not choose to make the proper noises to Grandmother. His lack of exuberance results from the fact that prizes which are won cheaply are of little value, regardless of the cost to the original purchaser.

There is another reason that the child should be denied some of the things he thinks he wants. Although it sounds paradoxical, you actually cheat him of pleasure when you give him too much. A classic example of this saturation principle is evident in my household each year during the Thanksgiving season. Our family is blessed with several of the greatest cooks who ever ruled a kitchen, and several times a year they do their "thing." The traditional Thanksgiving dinner consists of turkey, dressing, cranberries, mashed potatoes, sweet potatoes, peas, home-made hot rolls, two kinds of salad, and six or eight other dishes. Our behavior at this table is disgraceful, but wonderful. Everyone eats until he is uncomfortable, not saving room for dessert. Then the apple pie, pound cake, and fresh ambrosia are brought to the table. It just doesn't seem possible that we could eat another bite, yet somehow we do. Finally, taut family members begin to stagger away from their plates, looking for a place to fall. Later, about three o'clock in the afternoon, the internal pressure begins to subside, and someone passes the candy around. As the usual time for the evening meal arrives, no one is hungry, yet we've come to expect three meals a day. Turkey and roll sandwiches are constructed and consumed, followed by another helping of pie. By this time, everyone is a bit blank-eyed, absent-mindedly eating what they neither want nor enjoy. This ridiculous ritual continues for two or three days, until the thought of food becomes disgusting. Whereas eating ordinarily offers one of life's greatest pleasures, it loses its thrill when the appetite for food is satiated.

Pleasure occurs when an intense need is satisfied. If there is no need, there is no pleasure. A glass of water is worth more than gold to a man dying of thirst. The analogy to children should be obvious. If you never allow a child to want something, he never enjoys the pleasure of receiving it. If you buy him a tricycle before he can walk, and a bicycle before he can ride, and a car before he can drive, and a diamond ring before he knows the value of money, he accepts these gifts with little pleasure and less appreciation. How unfortunate that such a child never had the chance to long for something, dreaming about it at night and plotting for it by day. He might have even gotten desperate enough to work for it. The same possession that brought a yawn could have been a trophy and a treasure. I suggest that you and your wife allow your child the thrill of temporary deprivation; it's more fun and much less expensive.[13]

How can I teach my children Christian attitudes toward possessions and money?

This is accomplished not only with words, but also by the way you handle your own resources.

It is interesting to me that Jesus had more to say in the Bible about money than any other subject, which emphasizes the importance of this topic for my family and yours. He made it clear that there is a direct relationship between great riches and spiritual poverty, as we are witnessing in America today. Accordingly, it is my belief that excessive materialism in parents has the power to inflict enormous spiritual damage on our sons and daughters. If they see that we care more about things than people . . . if they perceive that we have sought to buy their love as a guilt reducer . . . if they recognize the hollowness of our Christian testimony when it is accompanied by stinginess with God . . . the result is often cynicism and disbelief. And more important, when they observe Dad working fifteen hours a day to capture ever more of this world's goods, they know where his treasure is. Seeing is believing.[14]

We've heard a lot about war toys. Do you think they are damaging to children?

Kids have been playing cowboys and Indians and other combat games for hundreds of years, and I'm inclined to feel that the current worry is unfounded. Young boys, particularly, live in a feminine world; they're with their mothers far more than their dads. The teachers of the nursery school, kindergarten, and elementary school are likely to be women. Their Sunday school teachers are probably female, too. In this sugar and spice world, I think it is healthy for boys to identify with masculine models, even if the setting involves combat. Two boys can "shoot" each other without emotional arousal. "Bang! Bang! You're dead," they shout.

On the other hand, parents should limit the amount of violence and killing their children view on television and in the movies. The technology of audio-visual electronics has become tremendously effective, and can be far more stimulating and damaging. Measurable physiological changes occur while a child is watching a violent movie; the pulse rate quickens, eyes dilate, hands sweat, the mouth goes dry, and breathing accelerates. If repeated often, the emotional impact of this experience should be obvious.[15]

My husband and I are distressed because our teenager seems to be rejecting her Christian beliefs. She was saved at an early age and in the past has shown a real love for the Lord. My inclination is to panic, but before I do, can you offer a word of encouragement?

A small child is told what to think during his formative years. He is subjected to all the attitudes, biases, and beliefs of his parents, which is right and proper. They are fulfilling their God-given responsibility to guide and train him. However, there must come a moment when all of these concepts and ideas are examined by the individual, and either adopted as true or rejected as false. If that personal evaluation never comes, then the adolescent fails to span the gap between "What I've been told" versus "What I believe." This is one of the most important bridges leading from childhood to adulthood.

It is common, then, for a teenager to question the veracity of the indoctrination he has received. He may ask himself, "Is there really a God? Does He know me? Do I believe in the values my parents have taught? Do I want what they want for my life? Have they misled me in any way? Does my experience contradict what I've been taught?" For a period of years beginning during adolescence and continuing into the twenties, this intensive self-examination is conducted.

This process is especially distressing to parents who must sit on the sidelines and watch everything they have taught being scrutinized and questioned. It will be less painful, however, if both generations realize that the soul-searching is a normal, necessary part of growing up.[16]

At what age should a child be given more freedom of choice regarding his religious beliefs and practices?
After the middle adolescent years (thirteen to sixteen years), some children resent being told exactly what to believe; they do not want religion "forced down their throats," and should be given more and more autonomy in what they believe. But if the early exposure has been properly conducted, they will have an inner mainstay to steady them. That early indoctrination, then, is the key to the spiritual attitudes they will carry into adulthood.

Despite this need to take a softer approach to spiritual training as the child moves through adolescence, it is *still* appropriate for parents to establish and enforce a Christian standard of behavior in their homes. Therefore, I *would* require my seventeen-year-old to attend church with the family. He should be told, "As long as you are under this roof, we will worship God together as a family. I can't control what you think. That's your business. But I have promised the Lord that we will honor Him in this home, and that includes 'remembering the Sabbath to keep it holy.'"[17]

You've indicated that seven deaths have occurred in your family during the past eighteen months. We have also had several tragic losses in our family in recent years. My

**wife died when our children were five, eight, and nine. I
found it very difficult to explain death to them during
that time. Can you offer some guidelines regarding how a
parent can help his children cope with the stark reality of
death—especially when it strikes within the immediate
family?**

Some years ago, I attended a funeral at the Inglewood
Cemetery-Mortuary in Inglewood, California. While there, I
picked up a brochure written by the president of the mortuary,
John M. McKinley. Mr. McKinley had been in the funeral
business for fifteen years before writing this valuable pamphlet
entitled "If It Happens to Your Child." He gave me permission to
reproduce the content here in answer to your question:

> I knew Tommy's parents because they lived in the
> neighborhood and attended the same church. But I knew
> Tommy especially well because he was one of the liveliest,
> happiest five-year-olds it had ever been my pleasure to
> meet. It was a shock, therefore, when his mother became a
> client of mine at the death of her husband.
>
> As a doctor must learn to protect himself from the
> suffering of his patients, so a funeral director must protect
> himself from grief. During the course of the average year I
> come in direct contact with several thousand men and
> women who have experienced a shattering loss, and if I did
> not isolate myself from their emotions, my job would be
> impossible. But I have not been able to isolate myself from
> the children.
>
> "I don't know what I would have done if I had not had
> Tommy," his mother told me when I visited her in her
> home the morning she called me. "He has been such a little
> man—hasn't cried, and is doing everything he can do to
> take his daddy's place." And it was true. Tommy was
> standing just as he imagined a man would stand, not
> crying, and doing his best to take his daddy's place.
>
> I knew it was wrong. I knew I should tell her so—that
> Tommy was not a man; that he needed to cry; that he
> needed comfort probably far more than she. But I am not a
> psychologist, and I said nothing.
>
> In the two years since then I have watched Tommy. The
> joy has not come back in his face, and it is clear even to my
> layman's mind that he is an emotionally sick child. I am
> sure it began when his mother, unknowingly, made it

difficult—impossible—for him to express his grief, and placed on him an obligation he could not fulfill; that of "taking daddy's place."

There have been few examples so clear cut as Tommy's, but I have seen so much that made me wince, and I have been asked so often: "What should I tell Mary?" or Paul, or Jim, that I finally decided to do something about it. I went to the experts, the men who know how a child should be treated at such moments of tragedy, and I asked them to lay down some guidelines that parents could understand and follow. I talked to several psychologists and psychiatrists and pediatricians, but principally to Dr. A. I. Duvall, a psychiatrist, and Dr. James Gardner, a child psychologist. Translated into my layman's language, here is the gist of what I learned.

—When a child, like any other human being, experiences a deeply painful loss, not only should he be permitted to cry; he should be encouraged to cry until the need for tears is gone. He should be comforted while the tears are flowing, but the words "Don't cry" should be stricken from the language.

—The need to cry may be recurrent for several days, or at widening intervals, several months; but when the need is felt, no effort should be made to dam the tears. Instead, it should be made clear that it is good to cry, and not "babyish" or "sissy" or anything to be ashamed of.

—At times, the child may need to be alone with his grief, and if this feeling comes, it should be respected. But otherwise physical contact and comfort will be almost as healing as the tears.

—The child should be told the truth; that death is final. "Mommy has gone on a vacation" or "Daddy has gone on a trip" only adds to the confusion and delays the inevitable. Children—particularly young children—have a very imperfect time sense. If "Mommy has gone on a vacation," they are going to expect her back this afternoon or tomorrow. And when tomorrow and tomorrow comes and she does not reappear, not only will the hurt be repeated endlessly, but the child will lose faith in the surviving parent just at the time when faith and trust are needed most. It is hard to say "never" when you know it will make the tears flow harder, but it is the kindest word in the long run.

—It is not necessary to explain death to a young child. It may even be harmful to try. To the five-year-old, "death" is absence, and explanations may only confuse him. If he has seen a dead bird or a dead pet, it may be helpful to make a comparison, but the important fact which the child must accept is absence. If he can be helped to accept the fact that father or mother or brother or sister is gone and will never return, then through questions and observations he will gradually build his own picture of "death" and its meaning.

—A child should not be unduly shielded from the physical appearance and fact of death. If a father dies, the child should be permitted to see the body, so that with his own eyes he can see the changes, the stillness, the difference between the vital strength which was "daddy" and this inanimate mask which is not "daddy" at all. Seeing with his own eyes will help.

—A child should be protected, however, from any mass demonstrations of grief, as from a large group of mourners at a funeral. Rather, the child should be taken in privately before the funeral to say goodbye.

—If the child is very young—say two to five or six—great care should be used in explaining death in terms which are meaningful to adults, but which may be very puzzling to children. For example, to say that "Mommy has gone to Heaven" may make perfect sense to a religious bereaved father, but it may leave a five-year-old wondering why Mommy has deserted him. At that answer, "Heaven" is simply a far place, and he will not be able to understand why his mother stays there instead of coming home to take care of him.

—Along with tears, a child is quite likely to feel sharp resentment, even anger at the dead parent, or the brother or sister who has "gone." This feeling is the result of the child's conviction that he has been deserted. If this feeling does arise, the child should be permitted to express it freely, just as in the case of tears.

—More common, and frequently more unsettling to a child, is his guilt feelings when a death occurs. If he has been angry at his sister, and the sister dies, he is likely to think it is his fault, that his anger killed her. Or if his mother dies, and he is not told honestly and simply what has happened, he is likely to believe that his misbehavior drove her away. Guilt feelings in young children, reinforced by death, can lead to neurotic patterns which last throughout life.

But if a child is encouraged to cry until the need for tears is gone; if he is comforted enough; if he is told the simple truth; if he is permitted to see for himself the difference between death and life; if his resentment or guilt is handled in the same straightforward way as his tears, his sense of loss will still be great, but he will overcome it.

There is a positive side, too. If death is treated as a natural part of human experience, it is much easier for a loved one to live in memory. When the initial impact of grief is gone, it is a natural thing to remember and re-tell stories which evoke vivid recollections of the personality and habits which made the loved one a special person. Children take great delight in this, for in their rich world of imagination they can make the absent one live again. Such reminiscing does not renew or increase their sorrow. To the extent that it makes them free to remember, the cause for sorrow is removed.

Mr. McKinley's advice is excellent, as far as it goes. However, it has not included any references to the Christian message, which provides the *only* satisfactory answer to death. Obviously, I disagree with Mr. McKinley's reservations about heaven. We can say, "Your mother is gone for now, but thank God we'll be together again on the other side!" How comforting for a grieving child to know that a family reunion will someday occur from which there will never be another separation! I recommend that Christian parents begin acquainting their children with the gift of eternal life long before they have need of this understanding.[18]

SECTION 3
EDUCATION OF CHILDREN

I've read that it is possible to teach four-year-old children to read. Should I be working on this with my child?

If a preschooler is particularly sharp and if he can learn to read without feeling undue adult pressure, it might be advantageous to teach him this skill. Those are big "if's," however. Few parents can work with their own children without showing frustration over natural failures. It's like teaching your wife to drive: risky, at best—disastrous at worst. Besides this limitation, learning should be programmed at the age when it is most needed. Why invest unending effort in teaching a child to read when he has not yet learned to cross the street, or tie his shoes, or count to ten, or answer the telephone? It seems foolish to get panicky over preschool reading, as such. The best policy is to provide your children with many interesting books and materials, to read to them and answer their questions, and then to let nature take its unobstructed course.[1]

Some educators have said we should eliminate report cards and academic marks. Do you think this is a good idea?

No, academic marks are valuable for students in the third grade or higher. They serve as a form of reinforcement—as a reward for the child who has achieved in school and as a nudge to the youngster who hasn't. It is important, though, that marks be used properly; they have the power to create or to destroy motivation. Through the elementary years and in the required courses of high school, a child's grades should be based on what he does with what he has. In other words, we should grade according to ability. A slow child should be able to succeed in school just as certainly as a gifted youngster. If he struggles and sweats to achieve, he should be rewarded with a symbol of accomplishment even if his work falls short of an absolute standard. By the same token, the gifted child should not be given an A just because he is smart enough to excel without working.

Our primary purpose in grading during the elementary and junior high school years should be to reward academic effort. On the other hand, college preparation courses in high school must be graded on an absolute standard. An A in chemistry or Latin is accepted by college admission boards as a symbol of excellence, and high school teachers must preserve that meaning. But then, Slow Joe and his friends need not be in those difficult courses.[2]

Do you ever favor removing a child from one school and transferring him to another?
Yes, there are times when a change of schools—or even a change of teachers within a school—can be in the child's best interest. Educators are reluctant to approve these transfers, for obvious reasons, although the possibility should be considered when the situation warrants. For example, there are occasions when a young student runs into social problems that can be resolved best by giving him a "clean start" somewhere else. Furthermore, schools vary tremendously in their difficulty; some are located in higher socioeconomic areas where a majority of the children are much more intelligent than would ordinarily be expected. The mean IQ in schools of this nature may fall between 115-120. What happens, then, to a child with average ability in such a setting? Although he might have competed successfully in an ordinary school, he is in the lower 15 percent at Einstein Elementary. My point is this: success is not absolute, it is relative. A child does not ask, "How am I doing?" but rather, "How am I doing compared to everyone else?" Little Johnny may grow up thinking he is a dummy when he would have been an intellectual leader in a less competitive setting. Thus, if a child is floundering in one academic environment, for *whatever* reason, the solution might involve a transfer to a more suitable classroom.[3]

Do you think religion should be taught in the public schools?

Not as a particular doctrine or dogma. The right of parents to select their child's religious orientation must be protected and no teacher or administrator should be allowed to contradict what the child has been taught at home. On the other hand, the vast majority of Americans do profess a belief in God. I would like to see this unnamed God acknowledged in the classroom. The Supreme Court decision banning nonspecific school prayer (or even silent prayer) is an extreme measure, and I regret it. The tiny minority of children from atheistic homes could easily be protected by the school during prayerful moments.

Incidentally, it is interesting to me that the courts have absolutely prohibited even silent prayer in the classroom, yet the Congress of the United States begins its session every day with spoken prayer. Likewise, the Supreme Court ruled in 1981 that schools could not even post the Ten Commandments on their bulletin boards, yet those same biblical directives are inscribed on the walls of the Supreme Court building! What does that tell us about the wisdom of our judges in establishing moral policy for the nation?[4]

I have observed that elementary school and junior high school students, even high schoolers, tend to admire the more strict teachers. Why is this true?

Yes, the teachers who maintain order *are* often the most respected members of the faculties, provided they aren't mean and grouchy. A teacher who can control a class without being oppressive is almost always loved by her students. One reason is that there is safety in order. When a class is out of control, particularly at the elementatary school level, the children are afraid of each other. If the teacher can't make the class behave, how can she prevent a bully from doing his thing? How can she keep the students from ridiculing one of its less able members? Children are not very fair and understanding with each other, and they feel good about having a strong teacher who is.

Second, children love justice. When someone has violated a rule, they want immediate retribution. They admire the teacher who can enforce an equitable legal system, and they find great comfort in reasonable social rules. By contrast, the teacher who does not control her class inevitably allows crime to pay, violating something basic in the value system of children.

Third, children admire strict teachers because chaos is nerve-racking. Screaming and hitting and wiggling are fun for about ten minutes; then the confusion begins to get tiresome and irritating.

I have smiled in amusement many times as second- and third-grade children astutely evaluated the relative disciplinary skills of their teachers. They know how a class should be conducted. I only wish all of their teachers were equally aware of this important attribute.

I am a teacher in junior high school, and there are five separate classes that come to my room to be taught science each day. My biggest problem is getting these students to bring books, paper, and pencils to class with them. I can lend them the equipment they need, but I never get it back. What do you suggest?

I faced an identical problem the years I taught in junior high school, and finally reached a solution which is based on the certainty that young people will cooperate if it is to *their* advantage to do so. After begging and pleading and exhorting them unsuccessfully, I announced one morning that I was no longer concerned about whether they brought their pencils and books to class. I had twenty extra books and several boxes of sharpened pencils which they could borrow. If they forgot to bring these materials, all they had to do was ask for a loan. I would not gnash my teeth or get red in the face; they would find me willing to share my resources. However, there was to be one hitch: the borrowing student would have to forfeit his seat for that one-hour class. He would have to stand by his chair while I was teaching, and if any written work was required, he had to lean over his desk from a standing position. As might be imagined, the students were less than ecstatic about this prospect. I smiled to myself and saw them racing around before class, trying to borrow a book or pencil. I did not have to enforce the standing rule very often because the issue had become the pupils' campaign rather than mine. Once a week, or so, a student would have to spend the hour in a vertical position, but that youngster made certain he did not blunder into the same situation twice.

The principle has broader applicability: give children maximum reason to *want* to comply with your wishes. Your anger is the *least* effective of all possible reasons.[5]

Do you think it would be useful to reinstate the traditional rules and regulations in the schools, such as dress codes, guidelines on hair length, and good grooming?

While I agree with the viewpoint that hair style and similar matters of momentary fashion are not worthy of concern in themselves, *adherence to a standard is an important element of discipline*. It is a great mistake to require *nothing* of children—to place no demands on their behavior. Whether a high school girl wears slacks or a dress is not of earthshaking importance, although it *is* significant that she be required to adhere to a few reasonable rules. If one examines the secret of success behind a championship football team, a magnificent orchestra, or a successful business, the principal ingredient is invariably discipline. How inaccurate is the belief that self-control is maximized in an environment which places no obligations on its children. How foolish is the assumption that self-discipline is a product of self-indulgence. *Reasonable* rules and standards are an important part of any educational system, in my view.[6]

I am a teacher of a wild fifth-grade class. In it are two or three kids who are driving me crazy. Can you offer some tips that will help me gain control?

Perhaps so. Let me offer these suggestions. First decide what is motivating the disruptive behavior: it takes no great social scientist to recognize that the loud mouths are usually seeking the attention of the group. For them, anonymity is the most painful experience imaginable. The ideal prescription is to extinguish their attention-getting behavior and then meet their need for gaining acceptance by less noisy means. I worked with a giddy little sixth grader named Larry whose mouth never shut. He perpetually disrupted the tranquility of his class, setting up a constant barrage of silliness, wise remarks, and horseplay. His teacher and I constructed an isolated area in a remote corner of the schoolroom; from that spot he could see nothing but his teacher and the front of the room. Thereafter, Larry was sentenced to a week in the isolation booth whenever he chose to be disruptive, which effectively eliminated the supporting reinforcement. Certainly, he could still act silly behind the screen, but he could not see the effect he was having on his peers. Besides this limitation, each outburst lengthened his lonely isolation. Larry spent one entire month in relative solitude before the extinction was finalized. When he rejoined society, his teacher immediately began to reward his cooperation. He was given the high status jobs (messenger, sergeant-at-arms, etc.) and praised for the improvement he had made. The results were remarkable.

Some school districts have implemented a more structured form of "extinction" for their worst behavioral problems (that is, the behavior is extinguished, not the children!). The students who are seemingly incapable of classroom cooperation are assigned to special classes, consisting of twelve to fifteen students. These youngsters are then placed on a program called "systematic exclusion." The parents are informed that the only way their child can remain in a public school is for them to come and get him if they are called during the school day. The child is then told that he can come to school each morning, but the moment he breaks one of the well-defined rules, he will be sent home. He might be ejected for pushing other pupils in the line at 9:01 A.M. Or he may make it until 1:15 or later before dismissal occurs. There are no second chances, although the child is free to return at the start of school the following morning. Despite the traditional belief that children hate school, most of them hate staying home even more. Daytime television gets pretty monotonous, particularly under the hostile eye of a mom who had to interrupt her activities to come get her wayward son. Disruptive behavior is very quickly extinguished under this controlled setting. It just isn't profitable for the student to challenge the system. Positive reinforcement in the form of verbal and material rewards are then generously applied for the child's attempts to learn and study. I worked with one child in a behavior modification classroom who was termed the most disruptive child ever seen at a major Los Angeles neuro-psychiatric hospital. After four months in this controlled setting, he was able to attend a regular class in the public schools.

All that is required to use this principle of extinction in a particular classroom is a little creativity and the administrative authority to improvise.[7]

It is my understanding that we forget 80 percent of everything we learn in three months' time and a higher percentage is forgotten as time passes. Why, then, should

**we put children through the agony of learning? Why is
mental exercise needed if the effort is so inefficient?**

Your question reflects the viewpoint of the old progressive
education theorists. They wanted the school curriculum to be
nothing more than "life adjustment." They placed a low priority
on intellectual discipline for the reasons you mentioned. Even
some college professors have adopted this "no content"
philosophy, reasoning that the material learned by students
today may be obsolete tomorrow, so why ask them to learn it? I
strongly disagree with this approach to education. There are at
least five reasons why learning is important, even if a high
incidence of forgetting and obsolescence do take place:

(1) Perhaps the most important function of school, apart from
teaching the basic literary and mathematical skills, is to foster
self-discipline and self-control. The good student learns to sit for
long hours, follow directions, carry out assignments and
channel his mental faculties. Homework, itself, is relatively
unnecessary as an educational tool, but it is valuable as an
instrument of discipline. Since adult life often requires
self-sacrifice, sweat, and devotion to causes, the school should
play a role in shaping a child's capacity to handle this future
responsibility. Certainly, play is important in a child's life too. He
should not work all the time; the home and school should
provide a healthy balance between discipline and play.

(2) Learning is important because we are *changed* by what we
learn, even if the facts are later forgotten. No college graduate
could remember everything he learned in school, yet he is a
very different person for having gone to college. Learning
produces alterations in values, attitudes, and concepts which do
not fade in time. (3) Even if the learned material cannot be
recalled, the individual knows the facts exist and where he can
find them. If we asked a complicated question of an uneducated
man, he would be likely to give a definite, unqualified response.
The same question would probably be answered more
cautiously by a man with a doctor's degree; he would say, "Well,
there are several ways to look at it." He knows the matter is
more complex than it appears, even if he doesn't have the full
answer. (4) We don't forget 100 percent of what we learn. The
most important facts take their place in our permanent memory
for future use. The human brain is capable of storing 2 billion
bits of data in a lifetime; education is the process of filling that
memory bank with useful information. (5) Old learning makes
new learning easier. Each mental exercise gives us more

associative cues with which to link future ideas and concepts.

I wish there were an easier, more efficient process for shaping human minds than the slow, painful experience of education. I'm afraid we'll have to depend on this old-fashioned approach until a "learning pill" is developed.[8]

The children who attend our church tend to be rather wild, and consequently, the classes are chaotic. Is this characteristic of most church school programs?

I'm afraid so, and it is a matter for concern. It has been my strong conviction that the church should support the family in its attempt to implement biblical principles in the home. This is especially true with reference to the teaching of respect for authority. This is not an easy time to be a parent because authority has eroded drastically in our society. Therefore, mothers and fathers who are trying to teach respect and responsibility to their children, as the Bible prescribes, need all the help they can get, particularly from the church.

But in my opinion, most churches fail miserably at this point. There is no aspect of the church mission that I feel is weaker or more ineffective than discipline in the Sunday school. Parents who have struggled to maintain order and respect all week send their kids off to church on Sunday morning, and what happens? They are permitted to throw erasers and shoot paper wads and swing on the light fixtures. I'm not referring to any one denomination. I've seen it happen in almost all of them. In fact, I think I was one of those eraser throwers in my day.[9]

Why do you think our Sunday schools are so lax and permissive, and what can we do about it?

Teachers are volunteers who may not know how to handle kids. But more often, they are afraid of irritating sensitive parents. They don't feel they have a right to teach children to respect God's house. If they try, they might anger Mama Bear and lose the entire family. I'm not recommending that we punish children in Sunday school, of course. But there are ways to maintain order among children, once we decide that it is important to us. Training sessions can help teachers do a better job. Pastors can back up Sunday school workers. Disruptive children can be assigned to a one-on-one relationship with a teacher for a time, etc. My concern is that we can't seem to agree

SECTION 4

LEARNING PROBLEMS IN CHILDHOOD

We have a one-year-old daughter and we want to raise her right. I've heard that parents can increase the mental abilities of their children if they stimulate them properly during the early years. Is this accurate, and if so, how can I accomplish this with my baby?

Recent research indicates that parents *can* increase the intellectual capability of their children. This conclusion was one of the most important findings derived from a ten-year study of children between eight and eighteen months of age. This investigation, known as Harvard University's Preschool Project, was guided by Dr. Burton L. White and a team of fifteen researchers between 1965 and 1975. They studied young children intensely during this period, hoping to discover which experiences in the early years of life contribute to the development of a healthy, intelligent human being. The conclusions from this exhaustive effort are summarized below, as reported originally in the *APA Monitor*.

1. It is increasingly clear that the origins of human competence are to be found in a critical period of development between eight and eighteen months of age. The child's experiences during these brief months do more to influence future intellectual competence than any time before or after.
2. The single most important environmental factor in the life of the child is his mother. "She is on the hook," said Dr. White, and carries more influence on her child's experiences than any other person or circumstance.
3. The amount of *live* language directed to a child

(not to be confused with television, radio, or overheard conversations) is vital to his development of fundamental linguistic, intellectual, and social skills. The researchers concluded, "Providing a rich social life for a twelve- to fifteen-month-old child is the best thing you can do to guarantee a good mind."

4. Those children who are given free access to living areas of their homes progressed much faster than those whose movements are restricted.

5. The nuclear family is the most important educational delivery system. If we are going to produce capable, healthy children, it will be by strengthening family units and by improving the interactions that occur within them.

6. The best parents were those who excelled at three key functions:

   (1) They were superb designers and organizers of their children's environments.

   (2) They permitted their children to interrupt them for brief thirty-second episodes, during which personal consultation, comfort, information, and enthusiasm were exchanged.

   (3) "THEY WERE FIRM DISCIPLINARIANS WHILE SIMUL-TANEOUSLY SHOWING GREAT AFFECTION FOR THEIR CHILDREN." (I couldn't have said it better myself.)[1]

These six conclusions are exciting to me, for I find within them an affirmation and validation of the scriptural concepts to which I have devoted my entire professional life: discipline with love; the dedication of mothers during the early years; the value of raising children; the stability of the family, etc. It is obvious that the Creator of the universe is best able to tell us how to raise children, and He has done just that through His holy Word.

Do you want to help your children reach the maximum potential that lies within them? Then raise them according to the precepts and values given to us in the Scriptures.[2]

My six-year-old son has always been an energetic child with some of the symptoms of hyperactivity. He has a short attention span and flits from one activity to another. I took him to a pediatrician who said he was not actually hyperactive, in the medical sense, and should

not be given medication for this mild problem. However, he's beginning to have learning problems in school because he can't stay in his seat and concentrate on his lessons. What should I do?

It is likely that your son is immature in comparison with his peers, a child we have traditionally called a "late bloomer." If so, he could profit from being retained in the first grade next year. If his birthday is between December 1 and July 1, I would definitely ask the school guidance office to advise you on this possibility. If that service is not available, you should have him examined for educational readiness by a child development specialist (child psychologist, pediatrician, neurologist, etc.). Retaining an immature boy during his early school career (kindergarten or first grade) can give him a great social and academic advantage throughout the remaining years of elementary school. However, it is very important to help him "save face" with his peers. If possible, he should change schools for at least a year to avoid embarrassing questions and ridicule from his former classmates.

Let me state my recommendation in broader terms for other parents of preschool children. The age of the child is the *worst* criterion on which to base a decision regarding when to begin a school career. That determination should be made according to specific neurologic, social, psychologic and pediatric variables. And for boys, who average six months behind girls of comparable age in maturity, it is even more important to consider his readiness to learn.

Finally, I agree with the perspective of Dr. Raymond Moore and Dorothy Moore regarding the value of postponing formalized education for *all* children. Writing in their excellent book, *Home Grown Kids* (Word Publishers), they provide irrefutable evidence to indicate that children who are kept at home until even eight or nine years of age, when finally enrolled in school, typically catch and pass their age mates within a few months. Furthermore, they are less vulnerable to the whims of the group and show long-term qualities of independence and leadership. Keeping children at home in the early elementary school years is an idea whose time has come. If further information is desired, I suggest that you read the Moores' interesting book on this subject.[3]

Can the late bloomer who is *not* retained or held out of school be expected to catch up with his class academically after he has matured physically?
Usually not. If the problem were simply a physical phenomenon, the slow maturing child could be expected to gain on his early developing friends. However, emotional factors are invariably tangled in this difficulty. A child's self-concept is amazingly simple to damage but exceedingly difficult to reconstruct. Once a child begins to think of himself as stupid, incapable, ignorant, and foolish, the concept is not easily eliminated. If he is unable to function as required in the early academic setting, he is compressed in the vise-like jaws of the school and the home; the conflict is often deeply ingrained.[4]

If age is such a poor factor to use in determining classroom readiness, why do schools use it exclusively to indicate when a child will enter kindergarten?
Because it is so convenient. Parents can plan for the definite beginning of school when their child reaches six years of age. School officials can survey their districts and know how many first graders they will have the following year. If an eight-year-old moves into the district in October, the administrator knows with certainty that the child belongs in the second grade, and so on. The use of chronological age as a criterion for school entrance is great for everybody—except the late bloomer.[5]

We have a six-year-old son who is also a late bloomer, and he is having trouble learning to read. Can you explain the link between his immaturity and this perplexing learning problem?
It is likely that your late bloomer has not yet completed a vital neurologic process involving an organic substance called myelin. At birth, the nervous system of the body is not insulated. That is why an infant is unable to reach out and grasp an object; the electrical command or impulse is lost on its journey from the brain to the hand. Gradually, a whitish substance (myelin) begins to coat the nerve fibers, allowing controlled muscular action to occur. Myelinization typically proceeds from the head downward and from the center of the body outward. In other words, a child can control the movement

of his head and neck before the rest of his body. Control of the shoulder precedes the elbow, which precedes the wrist, which precedes the large muscles in the hands, which precedes small muscle coordination of the fingers. This explains why elementary school children are taught block letter printing before they learn cursive writing; the broad strokes and lines are less dependent on minute finger control than the flowing curves of mature penmanship.

Since visual apparatus in humans is usually the last neural mechanism to be myelinated, your immature child may not have undergone this necessary developmental process by his present age of six years. Therefore, such a child who is extremely immature and uncoordinated may be neurologically unprepared for the intellectual tasks of reading and writing. Reading, particularly, is a highly complex neurological process. The visual stimulus must be relayed to the brain without distortion, where it should be interpreted and retained in the memory. Not all six-year-old children are equipped to perform this task. Unfortunately, however, our culture permits few exceptions or deviations from the established timetable. A six-year-old must learn to read or he will face the emotional consequences of failure.[6]

My child is having great trouble in school again this year. The psychologist said he is a "slow learner," and will probably always struggle academically. Please tell me what a "slow learner" is.

A slow learner is a child who has difficulty learning in school, and usually scores between 70 and 90 on tests of intelligence. These individuals comprise more than 20 percent of the total population. In many ways, the school children in this category face some serious challenges in their classroom. Of particular concern are the individuals with IQs in the lower range of the slow learner classification (70 to 80) who are virtually destined to have difficulties in school. No special education is available for them in most schools, although they are not appreciably different from the borderline retarded students. A "retarded" child with an IQ of 70 would probably qualify for the highly specialized and expensive educational program, including a smaller class, a specially trained teacher, audio-visual aids and a "no fail" policy. By contrast, a slow learning child with an IQ of 80 would usually receive no such advantages. He must compete in regular classes against the full range of students who are more capable than he. The concept of competition implies winners and losers; it is the slow learner who usually "loses."[7]

What causes a child to be a slow learner?

There are many hereditary, environmental, and physical factors which contribute to one's intellect, and it is difficult to isolate the particular influences. In some cases, however, accumulating evidence seems to indicate that dull normal intelligence and even borderline retardation can be caused by a lack of intellectual stimulation in the child's very early years. There appears to be a critical period during the first three to four years when the potential for intellectual growth must be seized. If the opportunity is missed, the child may never reach the capacity which had originally been available to him. The slow learning child can be one who has not heard adult language regularly; he has not been provided with interesting books and puzzles to occupy his sensory apparatus; he has not been taken to the zoo, the airport, or other exciting places; he has grown up with a minimum of daily training and guidance from adults. The lack of stimulation available to such a child may result in the failure of enzyme systems to develop properly in the brain.[8]

You said the slow learning child faces some special challenges at school. What, specifically, are those hurdles for him?

He is the child who "would if he could—but he can't." He will rarely, if ever, get the thrill of earning a "hundred" on his spelling test. He is the last child chosen in any academic game or contest. He often has the least sympathy from his teachers. He is no more successful in social activities than he is in academic pursuits, and the other children often reject him openly. Like the late bloomer, the slow learner gradually develops a crushing image of failure that distorts his self-concept and damages his ego. A colleague of mine overheard two intellectually handicapped students discussing their prospects with girls; one said, "I do OK until they find out I'm a retard." Obviously, this child was keenly aware of his diminished status. What better way is there to assassinate self-confidence in our children than to place 20 percent of them in a situation where excellence is impossible to achieve, where inadequacy is the daily routine, and where inferiority is a living reality? It is not surprising that such a child may become a mischievous tormentor in the third grade, a bully in the sixth, a loudmouth in junior high, and a dropout-delinquent in high school.[9]

Is retention in the same grade advisable for any child, other than the late bloomer? How about the slow learner?

There are some students who profit from a second year in the same grade level. The best guideline regarding failure to promote is this: retain the child for whom something will be *different* next year. A child who is sick for seven months in one academic year might profit from another run-through when he is healthy. And again, the late bloomer should be held back in kindergarten (or the first grade at the latest) to place him with youngsters of comparable development. For the slow learner, however, nothing will be changed. If he was failing the fourth grade in June, he will continue to fail the fourth grade in September. It is not often realized that the curricular content of each grade level is very similar to the year before and the year after. The same concepts are taught year after year; the students in each grade are taken a little farther, but much of the time is spent in review. The arithmetical methods of addition and subtraction, for example, are taught in the primary years, but considerable work is done on these tasks in the sixth grade, too. Nouns and verbs are taught repeatedly for several years.

Thus, the most unjustifiable reason for retention is to give the slow learner another year of exposure to easier concepts. He will not do better the second time around! Nor is there much magic in summer school. Some parents hope that a six-week program in July and August will accomplish what was impossible in the ten months between September and June. They are often disappointed.[10]

If retention and summer school do not solve the problem of the slow learner, what can be done for these children?

Let me offer three suggestions that can tip the scales in favor of the slow learning child with learning problems.

1. *Teach him to read, even if a one-to-one teacher-student ratio is required* (and it probably will be). Nearly every child can learn to read, but many boys and girls have difficulty if taught

only in large groups. Their minds wander and they do not ask questions as readily. Certainly, it would be expensive for the school to support an additional number of remedial reading teachers, but I can think of no expenditure that would be more helpful. Special techniques, teaching machines and individual reinforcement can be successful in teaching reading—the most basic of all academic skills—to the children who are least likely to learn without individual attention. This assistance should not be delayed until the fourth or fifth grades or in junior high. By those late dates the child has already endured the indignities of failure.

Many school districts have implemented creative programs to focus on reading problems. One such program, the "ungraded primary," eliminates the distinctions between students in the first three grades. Instead of grouping children by age, they are combined according to reading skill. Good readers in the first, second, and third grade may occupy the same classes. Poor readers are also grouped together. This procedure takes the sting out of retention and allows children to profit from the benefits of homogeneous grouping. Another system is called the "split reading" program. In this method, the better half of the readers in a given class arrive at school thirty minutes early to be taught reading. The poorer half of the readers remain a half-hour later each evening for the same purpose. There are many such programs which have been devised to teach reading more effectively. And of course, parents who are concerned about their child's basic academic skills may wish to seek tutorial assistance to supplement these school programs.

Let me state it more explicitly: *It is absolutely critical to your child's self-concept that he learn to read early in his school career, and if professional educators can't do the job, someone else must!*

2. *Remember that success breeds success.* The best motivation for a slow learner is to know that he is succeeding. If the adults in his life show confidence in him, he will be more likely to have confidence in himself. In fact, most humans share this same characteristic. We tend to act the way we think other people "see" us. This reality was made clear to me when I joined the National Guard. I had recently graduated from college and chose to enlist for an extended period of reserve military experience rather than to serve two years of active duty. I was immediately packed up and put on a bus for Fort Ord, California, to undergo a six-month clerical training program.

Contrary to the recruiting posters, this exciting new career opportunity was not a matter of personal choice; it was selected for me. Nevertheless, the next six months were spent learning the fascinating world of military forms, typing, and filing. One hundred eighty-three days later I returned to the local National Guard unit with this newly acquired knowledge available for usage. Surprisingly, I was not welcomed back with any overwhelming degree of enthusiasm. Everyone knows that privates are stupid. *All* privates are stupid. I was a private, so it stood to reason that there was thickness between my ears. With the exception of a few other stupid privates, I was outranked by the whole world. Everybody from the privates-first-class to the colonel anticipated ignorant behavior from me, and to my amazement, their expectation proved accurate. The first assignment given, following six months of clerical training, was to type a simple letter in two copies. After investing twenty-five minutes of concentrated effort at the typewriter, I realized that the carbon paper was inserted upside down. Reverse lettering was smudged all over the back of the main copy, which did not exactly overwhelm the first sergeant with gratitude. Similar complex procedures, like marching "in step," were strangely difficult to perform. From today's perspective, it is clear that my performance was consistent with my image. Likewise, many children who fail in school are merely doing what they think others expect of them. Our reputation with our peers is a very influential force in our lives.

Finally, the slow learner needs individual attention in all of his academic work, which can only be given by teachers who have relatively small classes. He also needs access to audio-visual approaches to learning, including the latest in computer technology. The inordinate expense of such programs is a reality we must face in view of the current financial crisis in the schools, but for the slow learner, his program is dependent on receiving an enriched experience that does not often occur in the traditional classroom.[11]

Do slow learners and mentally retarded children have the same needs for esteem that others have?
Sometimes I wish they didn't, but their needs are no different. During a portion of my training at Lanternman State Hospital, Pomona, California, I was impressed by the vast need for love shown by some of the most retarded patients. There were times

when I would step into the door of a children's ward and forty or more severely retarded youngsters would rush toward me screaming, "Daddy! Daddy! Daddy!" They would push and shove around my legs with their arms extended upward, making it difficult to avoid falling. Their deep longings to be loved simply couldn't be satisfied in the group experiences of hospital life, despite the exceptionally high quality of Lanternman.

The need for esteem has led me to favor a current trend in education, whereby borderline mentally retarded children are given special assistance *in* their regular classrooms without segregating them in special classes. The stigma of being a "retard," as they call themselves, is no less insulting for a ten-year-old than it would be for you or me.[12]

I have heard the term "classic underachiever" applied to children—will you define that concept for me?

The underachiever is a student who is unsuccessful in school *despite* his ability to do the work. He may have an IQ of 120 or better, yet earn D's and F's on his report card. If possible, underachieving children are even more numerous and less understood than slow learners or late bloomers. The confusion is related to the fact that *two* specific ingredients are necessary to produce academic excellence, yet the second is often overlooked. First *intellectual ability* must be there. But mental capacity is insufficient by itself. *Self-discipline* is also required. An able child may or may not have the self-control necessary to bear down day after day on something he considers painful and difficult. Furthermore, intelligence and self-discipline are frequently *not* correlated. We often see a child having one without the other.[13]

What solution would you offer for the problem of underachievers?

I have dealt with more than 500 underachievers and have come to the conclusion that there are only two functional solutions to this syndrome. The first is certainly no panacea: parents can become so involved in schoolwork that the child has no choice but to do the job. To make this possible, the school must expend additional effort to communicate assignments and progress to parents—Junior is certainly not going to carry the message! Adolescents, particularly, will confound the communication between school and home as much as possible. In one of the high schools where I served, for example, students had a twenty-minute "homeroom" session each day. This time was used for the flag salute, council meetings, announcements, and related matters. Very little opportunity for studying occurred there, yet each day, hundreds of parents were told that all homework was finished during that session. The naive parents were led to believe that the homeroom period was a two-hour block of concentrated effort.

Parents must know what goes on in school if they want to reinforce their child's academic responsibilities. They should provide support in areas where self-discipline is needed. The evening study period should be highly structured—routine hours and a minimum of interferences. To do this, parents must know what was assigned and how the finished product should look. Finally, negative attitudes should be withheld from the learning situation. Berating and criticizing an underachiever do not make him work harder.

I must hasten to say that this procedure is not an easy solution. It rarely works for more than a week or two, since many parents also lack the required self-discipline to continue the program. And when they quit, so does Junior! There must be a better way, and I believe there is.

An underachiever often thrives under a system of immediate reinforcement.[14] If he is not challenged by personal satisfaction and motivators usually generated in the classroom, he must be fed some artificial incentives in the form of rewards applied to small units of behavior. Instead of gifts or other desirable objectives being offered to the child for earning an A in English at the end of the semester, he should be given ten cents for each properly diagrammed sentence.

The use of immediate reinforcement serves the same function as a starter on a car! You can't drive very far with it, but it gets the engine going much easier than pushing. For the idealist who objects to the use of the extrinsic motivation (which is often inaccurately called a bribe), I would ask this question: "What alternative do we have, other than to let the child grow out of his problem?"[15]

My child has a visual-perceptual problem that makes it hard for him to read. I understand his difficulty. But he brings home F's and D's in most of his classes, and I know that will limit his opportunities in life. What should be the attitude of a parent toward a child who fails year after year?

Obviously, tutorial assistance and special instruction should be provided, if possible. Beyond that, however, I would strongly suggest that academic achievement be de-emphasized at home.

Requiring a visually handicapped child or a slow learner to compete academically is like forcing a polio victim to run the hundred yard dash. Imagine a mother and father standing disapprovingly at the end of the track, berating their crippled child as he hobbles across the finish line in last place.

"Why don't you run faster, son?" his mother asks with obvious displeasure.

"I don't think you really care whether you win or lose," says his embarrassed father.

How can this lad explain that his legs will not carry him as fast as those of his peers? All he knows is that the other sprinters run past him to the cheering of the crowd. But who would expect a crippled child to win a race against healthy peers? No one, simply because his handicap is obvious. Everyone can see it.

Unfortunately, the child with a learning deficit is not so well understood. His academic failure is more difficult to understand and may be attributed to laziness, mischievousness, or deliberate defiance. Consequently, he experiences pressures to do the impossible. And one of the most serious threats to emotional health occurs when a child faces demands that he cannot satisfy.

Let me restate the preceding viewpoint in its most concise terms: I believe in academic excellence. I want to maximize every ounce of intellectual potential which a child possesses. I don't believe in letting him behave irresponsibly simply because he doesn't choose to work. Without question, there is a lasting benefit to be derived from educational discipline.

But, on the other hand, some things in life are more important than academic excellence, and self-esteem is one of them. A child can survive, if he must, without knowing a noun from a verb. But if he doesn't have some measure of self-confidence and personal respect, he won't have a chance in life.

I want to assert my conviction that the child who is

unequipped to prosper in the traditional educational setting is not inferior to his peers. He possesses the same degree of human worth and dignity as the intellectual young superstar. It is a foolish cultural distortion that causes us to evaluate the worth of children according to the abilities and physical features they may (or may not) possess.

Every child is of equal worth in the sight of God, and that is good enough for me. Thus, if my little boy or girl can't be successful in one environment, we'll just look for another. Any loving parent would do the same.[16]

Author's note: For a discussion of learning problems associated with visual-perceptual difficulties, see the section devoted to the topic, "Hyperactivity in Children."

SECTION 5

SEX EDUCATION AT HOME AND SCHOOL

When do children begin to develop a sexual nature? Does this occur suddenly during puberty?
No, it occurs long before puberty. Perhaps the most important scientific fact suggested by Freud was his observation that children are not asexual. He stated that sexual gratification begins in the cradle and is first associated with feeding. Behavior during childhood is influenced considerably by sexual curiosity and interest, although the happy hormones do not take full charge until early adolescence. It is not uncommon for a four-year-old to be fascinated by nudity and the sexual apparatus of boys versus girls. This is an important time in the forming of sexual attitudes; parents should be careful not to express shock and extreme disapproval of this kind of curiosity, although they are entitled to inhibit overt sexual activity between children. It is believed that many sexual problems begin as a result of inappropriate training during early childhood.[1]

Who should teach children about sex and when should that instruction begin?
For those parents who are able to handle the instructional process correctly, the responsibility for sex education should be retained in the home. There is a growing trend for all aspects of education to be taken from the hands of parents (or the role is deliberately forfeited by them). This is unwise. Particularly in the matter of sex education, the best approach is one that begins in early childhood and extends through the years, according to a policy of openness, frankness, and honesty. Only parents can provide this lifetime training.

The child's needs for information and guidance can rarely be met in one massive conversation provided by reluctant parents as their child approaches adolescence. Nor does a concentrated formal educational program outside the home offer the same advantages derived from a *gradual* enlightenment that begins during the third or fourth year of life and reaches a culmination shortly before puberty.[2]

Neither my husband nor I feel comfortable about discussing sex with our children. He thinks the school should supply the information they need, but I feel that it is our responsibility. Must I force myself to talk about this difficult subject?

Despite the desirability of sex education being handled by highly skilled parents, we have to face the fact that many families feel as you do. They are admittedly unqualified and reluctant to do the job. Their own sexual inhibitions make it extremely difficult for them to handle the task with poise and tact. For families such as yours which cannot teach their children the details of human reproduction, there must be outside agencies that will assist them in this important function. It is my firm conviction that the Christian church is in the best position to provide that support for its members, since it is free to teach not only the anatomy and physiology of reproduction, but also the *morality and responsibility* of sex. Unfortunately, most churches are also reluctant to accept the assignment, leaving the public schools as the only remaining resource.[3]

Do you believe in the "double standard," whereby girls are expected to remain virgins while boys are free to experiment sexually?

I most certainly do not. There is no such distinction found in the Bible, which must be the standard by which morality is measured. Sin is sin, whether committed by males or females.

We've been very slow getting around to sex education in our family. In fact, our child is eleven now, and we haven't given her any specific instructions. Is it too late, or is there still time to prepare her for adolescence?

Your situation is not ideal, of course, but you should do your best to help your daughter understand what the next few years will bring. Parents should usually plan to end their instructional program before their child enters puberty (the time of rapid sexual development in early adolescence). Puberty usually begins between ten and twelve years of age for girls and between twelve and fourteen for boys. Once this developmental period is entered, teenagers are typically embarrassed by discussions of sex with their parents. Adolescents usually resent adult intrusion during this time, preferring to have the subject of sex ignored at home. We should respect their wishes. We are given but a single decade to provide the proper understanding of human sexuality; after that foundation has been constructed, we can only serve as resources to whom the child can turn if he chooses.[4]

What should I talk about when I discuss sex with my preteenager?

In preparing yourself for these discussions, it may be helpful to review the checklist of ten subjects cited below. You should have a good notion of what you will say about each of these topics:

1. The role of intercourse in marriage
2. Male and female anatomy and physiology
3. Pregnancy and the birth process
4. Nocturnal emission ("wet dreams")
5. Masturbation
6. Guilt and sexual fantasy
7. Menstruation
8. Morality and responsibility in sex
9. Venereal disease
10. Secondary sex characteristics which will be brought about by glandular changes—pubic hair, general sexual development, increasing interest in sex, etc.[5]

How do you feel about sex education in the public schools, as it is typically handled?

For the children of Christian families or others with firm convictions about moral behavior, an acceptable sex education program must consist of two elements. First the anatomy and physiology of reproduction should be taught. Second, moral attitudes and responsibilities related to sex must be discussed.

These components should never be separated as long as the issue of morality is considered important! Sexual sophistication without sexual responsibility is sexual disaster! To explain all the mechanics of reproduction without teaching the proper attitudes and controls is like giving a child a loaded gun without showing him how to use it. Nevertheless, this second responsibility is often omitted or minimized in the public school setting.

Despite their wish to avoid the issue of morality, teachers of sex education find it almost impossible to remain neutral on the subject. Students will not allow them to conceal their viewpoint. "But what do you think about premarital intercourse, Mr. Burgess?" If Mr. Burgess refuses to answer this question, he has inadvertently told the students that there is no definite right or wrong involved. By not taking a stand for morality he has endorsed promiscuity. The issue appears arbitrary to his students, rendering it more likely that their intense biological desires will get satisfied.

I would like to stress the fact that I am not opposed to sex education in the public schools—provided both elements of the subject are presented properly. However, I don't want my children taught sex technology by a teacher who is either neutral or misinformed about the consequences of immorality. It would be preferable that Junior would learn his concepts in the streets than for a teacher to stand before his class, having all the dignity and authority invested in him by the school and society, and tell his impressionable students that traditional morality is either unnecessary or unhealthy. Unless the schools are prepared to take a definite position in favor of sexual responsibility (and perhaps the social climate prevents their doing so), some other agency should assist concerned parents in the provision of sex education for their children. As indicated earlier, churches could easily provide this service for society. The YMCA, YWCA, or other social institutions might also be helpful at this point. Perhaps there is no objective that is more important to the future of our nation than the teaching of moral discipline to the most recent generation of Americans.[6]

A recent book for parents contends that good sex education will reduce the incidence of promiscuity and sexual irresponsibility among teenagers. Do you agree?
Of course not. Teenagers are sexually better informed today

than at any time in human history, although the traditional boy-girl game seems to be as popular as ever. The assumption that physiologic information will inhibit sexual activity is about as foolish as thinking an overweight glutton can be helped by understanding the biologic process of eating. I am in favor of proper sex education for other reasons—but I have no illusions about its unique power to install responsibility in adolescents. Morality, if it is valued, must be approached directly, rather than through the back doors of anatomy and physiology. Of much greater potency is a lifelong demonstration of morality in all its forms by parents whose very lives reveal their fidelity and commitment to one another and to Jesus Christ.[7]

How do you feel about the teaching of traditional male and female roles to children? Do you think boys should be made to do girls' work, and vice versa?

The trend toward the blending of masculine and feminine roles is well ingrained in America at this time. Women smoke cigars and wear pants. Men splash perfume and don jewelry. There is little sexual identity seen in their hair length, manner, interests, or occupations, and the trend is ever more in this direction. Such similarity between men and women causes great confusion in the minds of children with regard to their own sex-role identity. They have no distinct models to imitate and are left to grope for the appropriate behavior and attitudes.

Therefore, I *firmly* believe in the value of teaching traditional male and female roles during the early years. To remove this prescribed behavior for a child is to further damage his sense of identity, which needs all the help it can get. The masculine and feminine roles are taught through clothing, close identification with the parent of the same sex, and, to some degree, through the kind of work required, and in the selection of toys provided for play. I am not suggesting that we panic over tomboy tendencies in our girls or that we demand he-man behavior from our boys. Nor is it unacceptable for a boy to wash the dishes or a girl to clean the garage. We should, on the other hand, gently nudge our children in the direction of their appropriate sex roles.[8]

Many American colleges and universities are permitting men and women to live in coeducational dormitories, often rooming side by side. Others now allow unrestricted

visiting hours by members of the opposite sex. Do you think this promotes more healthy attitudes toward sex?
It certainly promotes more sex, and some people think that's healthy. The advocates of cohabitation try to tell us that young men and women can live together without doing what comes naturally. That is nonsense. The sex drive is one of the strongest forces in human nature, and Joe College is notoriously weak in suppressing it. I would prefer that the supporters of coeducational dormitories admit that morality is not very important to them. If morality is something we value, then we should at least give it a wobbly-legged chance to survive. The sharing of collegiate bedrooms hardly takes us in that direction.[9]

THE DISCIPLINE OF INFANTS AND TODDLERS

**Some psychologists, especially the behaviorists, believe
that children are born as "blank slates," being devoid of
personality until they interact with their environments.
Do you agree?**

No. I am now certain that the personalities of newborns vary
tremendously, even before parental and environmental
influence is exercised. Every mother of two or more children
will affirm that each of her infants had a different personality—a
different "feel"—from the first time they were held. Numerous
authorities in the field of child development now agree that
these complex little creatures called babies are far from "blank
slates" when they enter the world. One important study by
Chess, Thomas, and Birch revealed nine kinds of behaviors in
which babies differ from one another. These differences tend to
persist into later life and include level of activity, respon-
siveness, distractibility, and moodiness, among others.

Another newborn characteristic (not mentioned by Chess) is
most interesting to me and relates to a feature which can be
called "strength of the will." Some children seem to be born with
an easygoing, compliant attitude toward external authority. As
infants they don't cry very often and they sleep through the
night from the second week and they goo at the grandparents
and they smile while being diapered and they're very patient
when dinner is overdue. During later childhood, they love to
keep their rooms clean and they especially like to do their
homework and they can entertain themselves for hours. There
aren't many of these supercompliant children, I'm afraid, but
they are known to exist in some households (not my own).

Just as surely as some children are naturally compliant, there

are others who seem to be defiant upon exit from the womb.
They come into the world smoking a cigar and yelling about the
temperature in the delivery room and the incompetence of the
nursing staff and the way things are run by the administrator of
the hospital. They expect meals to be served the instant they are
ordered, and they demand every moment of mother's time. As
the months unfold, their expression of willfulness becomes even
more apparent, the winds reaching hurricane force during
toddlerhood.

The expression of the will, whether compliant or defiant, is
only one of an infinite number of ways children differ at birth.
And how foolish of us to have thought otherwise. If God can
make every snowflake unique, and every grain of sand at the
beach is different from its counterparts, then why would the
Creator stamp out children as though they were manufactured
by Henry Ford? Hardly! Every one of us as human beings is
known to the Creator apart from every other human on earth.
And I'm thankful that we are![1]

**If children differ in temperament at the moment of birth,
then is it reasonable to conclude that some babies are
more difficult to care for than others?**

There *are* easy babies and there are difficult babies! Some seem
determined to dismantle the homes into which they were born;
they sleep cozily during the day and then howl in protest all
night; they get colic and spit up the vilest stuff on their clothes
(usually on the way to church); they control their internal
plumbing until you hand them to strangers, and then let it
blast. Instead of cuddling into the fold of the arms when being
held, they stiffen rigidly in search of freedom. And to be honest,
a mother may find herself leaning sockeyed over a vibrating
crib at 3:00 A.M., asking the eternal question, "Is this what my
life has come down to?" A few days earlier she was wondering,
"Will he survive?" Now she is asking, "Will *I* survive?"

But believe it or not, both generations will probably recover
and this disruptive beginning will be nothing but a dim memory
for the parents in such a brief moment. And from that
demanding tyrant will grow a thinking, loving human being
with an eternal soul and a special place in the heart of the
Creator. To the exhausted and harassed new mother, let me say,
"Hang tough! You are doing *the* most important job in the
universe."[2]

What kind of discipline is appropriate for my six-month-old son?

No *direct* discipline is necessary for a child under seven months of age, regardless of behavior or circumstances. Many parents do not agree, and find themselves "swatting" a child of six months for wiggling while being diapered or for crying in the midnight hours. This is a serious mistake. A baby is incapable of comprehending his "offense" or associating it with the resulting punishment. At this early age he needs to be held, loved, and most important, to hear a soothing human voice. He should be fed when hungry and kept clean and dry and warm. In essence, it is probable that the foundation for emotional and physical health is laid during this first six-month period, which should be characterized by security, affection, and warmth.[3]

I have a very fussy eight-month-old baby who cries whenever I put her down. My pediatrician says she is healthy and that she cries just because she wants me to hold her all the time. I do give her a lot of attention, but I simply can't keep her on my lap all day long. How can I make her less fussy?

The crying of infants is an important form of communication. Through their tears we learn of their hunger, fatigue, discomfort, or diaper disaster. Thus, it is important to listen to those calls for help and interpret them accordingly. On the other hand, your pediatrician is right. It *is* possible to create a fussy, demanding baby by rushing to pick her up every time she utters a whimper or sigh. Infants are fully capable of learning to manipulate their parents through a process called reinforcement, whereby any behavior that produces a pleasant result will tend to recur. Thus, a healthy baby can keep his mother hopping around his nursery twelve hours a day (or night) by simply forcing air past his sandpaper larynx. To avoid this consequence, it is important to strike a balance between giving your baby the attention she needs and establishing her as a tiny dictator. Don't be afraid to let her cry a reasonable period of time (which is thought to be healthy for the lungs), although it is necessary to listen to the tone of her voice for the difference between random discontent and genuine distress. Most mothers learn to recognize this distinction in time.

I used to stand out of sight at the doorway of my daughter's nursery for four or five minutes, awaiting a momentary lull in the crying before going to her crib. By so doing, I reinforced the pauses rather than the tears. You might try the same approach.

Perhaps it would be helpful to illustrate this point by including a letter which reached my desk recently.

Dear Dr. Dobson:

The reason I'm writing is this: The Lord has blessed us so much I should be full of joy. But I have been depressed for about ten months now. I don't know whether to turn to a pastor, a doctor, a psychologist, a nutritionist, or a chiropractor!

Last September the Lord gave us a beautiful baby boy. He is just wonderful. He is cute and he is smart and he is strong. We just can't help but love him. But he has been very demanding. The thing that made it hardest for me was last month Jena was taking some college classes two nights a week, and I took care of Rolf. He cried and sobbed the whole time and eventually cried himself to sleep. Then I would either hold him because he would awaken and continue crying, or if I did get to lay him down, I wouldn't make any noise because I was afraid I would wake him up.

I am used to being able to pay bills, work on the budget, read and file mail, answer letters, type lists, etc., in the evening. But all this must be postponed to a time when Jena is here.

That's why it has been such a depressing time for me. I just can't handle all that crying. It is probably worse because Jena is breast feeding Rolf. That wakes me up too, and I get very tired and am having a great deal of trouble getting up in the morning to go to work. Now I have started getting sick very easily.

I love our baby a lot and wouldn't trade him for anything in the world, but I don't understand why I'm so depressed. Sure Jena gets tired too because we can't seem to get Rolf to go down for the night before 11 or 12 midnight and he wakes up twice in every night.

Another thing that has been a constant struggle is leaving Rolf in the nursery at church. He isn't content to be away from us very long so the workers end up having to track Jena down almost every week. We hardly ever get to be together for the worship service. And this has been going on for ten months!

We have all the things we would ever dream of at our age — our own neat little house in a good neighborhood, a good job that I enjoy, and not least of all, our life in Christ.

I have no reason to be depressed and to be so tired all the time. I come home from work so exhausted that I'm in no frame of mind to take Rolf out of his mother's hair so she can fix dinner. He hangs on her all the time. I just don't know how she stands it. She must have a higher tolerance to frustration than I do.

If you have any insights as to what we should do, please let me know. Thanks, and God bless you!

Chuck

It is difficult to believe that a ten-month-old baby could take complete charge of two mature adults and mold them to suit his fancy, but that is precisely what Rolf is doing. He fits the pattern of an extremely strong-willed baby who has already learned how to manipulate his parents to achieve his purposes. If they put him to bed or even set him down, if they leave him in the nursery, if they turn their backs on him for a moment—he screams in protest. And being peace-loving parents with great needs for solitude and tranquility, they jump to satisfy Rolf's noisy demands before he gets agitated. In so doing, they "reinforce" his tearful behavior and guarantee its continuation.

I would recommend that Chuck and Jena feed and diaper Rolfie, then proceed to let him cry himself to sleep at about 7:00 P.M. every evening for a week. As this little fellow becomes convinced that the exhausting work of continuous crying is not going to accomplish his objectives, the behavior will disappear. Likewise, they should give him plenty of love and attention and then go about their duties and activities. Rolf will get the message in time.

On the other hand, if Rolfie is, as I suspect, a bona fide strong-willed child, his parents can anticipate a few hundred-thousand more struggles on other battlefields in the years to come.[4]

Please describe the best approach to the discipline of a one-year-old child.
Many children will begin to test the authority of their parents during the second seven-month period. The confrontations will

be minor and infrequent before the first birthday, yet the beginnings of future struggles can be seen. My own daughter, for example, challenged her mother for the first time when she was nine months old. My wife was waxing the kitchen floor when Danae crawled to the edge of the linoleum. Shirley said, "No, Danae," gesturing to the child not to enter the kitchen. Since our daughter began talking very early, she clearly understood the meaning of the word *no*. Nevertheless, she crawled straight onto the sticky wax. Shirley picked her up and set her down in the doorway, while saying, "No" more firmly. Not to be discouraged, Danae again scrambled onto the newly mopped floor. My wife took her back, saying, "No" even more strongly as she put her down. Seven times this process was repeated until Danae finally yielded and crawled away in tears. As far as we can recall, that was the first direct collision of wills between my daughter and wife. Many more were to follow.

How does a parent discipline a one-year-old? Very carefully and gently! A child at this age is extremely easy to distract and divert. Rather than jerking a wrist watch from his hands, show him a brightly colored alternative—and then be prepared to catch the watch when it falls. When unavoidable confrontations do occur, as with Danae on the waxy floor, win them by firm persistence but not by punishment. Again, don't be afraid of the child's tears, which can become a potent weapon to avoid naptime or bedtime or diapertime. Have the courage to lead the child without being harsh or mean or gruff.

Compared to the months that are to follow, the period around one year of age is usually a tranquil, smooth-functioning time in a child's life.[5]

Are the "terrible twos" really so terrible?

It has been said that all human beings can be classified into two broad categories: those who would vote "yes" to the various propositions of life, and those who would be inclined to vote "no." I can tell you with confidence that each toddler around the world would definitely cast a negative vote! If there is one word that characterizes the period between fifteen and twenty-four months of age, it is *no!* No, he doesn't want to eat his cereal. No, he doesn't want to play with his dump truck. No, he doesn't want to take his bath. And you can be sure, no, he doesn't want to go to bed anytime at all. It is easy to see why this period of life has been called "the first adolescence," because of the negatives, conflict, and defiance of the age.

Perhaps the most frustrating aspect of the "terrible twos" is the tendency of kids to spill things, destroy things, eat horrible things, fall off things, flush things, kill things, and get into things. They also have a knack for doing embarrassing things, like sneezing on a nearby man at a lunch counter. During these toddler years, any unexplained silence of more than thirty seconds can throw an adult into a sudden state of panic. What mother has not had the thrill of opening the bedroom door, only to find Tony Tornado covered with lipstick from the top of his pink head to the carpet on which he stands? On the wall is his own artistic creation with a red handprint in the center, and throughout the room is the aroma of Chanel No. 5 with which he has anointed his baby brother. Wouldn't it be interesting to hold a national convention sometime, bringing together all the mothers who have experienced that exact trauma?

The picture sounds bleak, and, admittedly, there are times when a little toddler can dismantle the peace and tranquility of a home. (My son Ryan loved to blow bubbles in the dog's water dish—a game which still horrifies me.) However, with all of its struggles, there is no more thrilling time of life than this period of dynamic blossoming and unfolding. New words are being learned daily, and the cute verbal expressions of that age will be remembered for half a century. It is a time of excitement over fairy stories and Santa Claus and furry puppy dogs. And most important, it is a precious time of loving and warmth that will scurry by all too quickly. There are millions of older parents today with grown children who would give all they possess to relive those bubbly days with their toddlers.[6]

It is already obvious that we have an extremely defiant child who has demanded his own way since the day he was born. I think we have disciplined and trained him as well as possible, but he still opposes any boundaries or limits we try to set on him. Can you tell me why *I* feel so guilty and defeated, even though I know I've been a good parent? Your guilt is very common among parents of strong-willed children, and for good reason. You are engaged in an all-out tug of war which leaves you frustrated and fatigued. No one told you that parenthood would be this difficult, and you blame yourself for the tension that arises. You and your husband had planned to be such loving and effective parents, reading fairy stories to your pajama-clad angels by the fireplace. But reality has turned out to be quite different, and that difference is depressing to you.

Furthermore, I have found that the parents of compliant children don't understand their friends with defiant youngsters. They intensify guilt and anxiety by implying, "If you would raise your kids the way I do it, you wouldn't be having those awful problems." May I emphasize to both groups that the willful child can be difficult to control even when his parents handle him with great skill and dedication.

Our twenty-four-month-old son is not yet toilet trained, although my mother-in-law feels he should be under control now. Should we spank him for using his pants instead of the potty?
No. Tell your mother-in-law to cool down a bit. It is entirely possible that your child *can't* control himself at this age. The last thing you want to do is spank a two-year-old for an offense which he can't comprehend. If I had to err on this matter, it would be in the direction of being too late with my demands, rather than too early. Furthermore, the best approach to potty training is with rewards rather than with punishment. Give him a sucker (or sugarless candy) for performing properly. When you've proved that he can comply, then you can hold him responsible in the future.[7]

I get very upset because my two-year-old boy will not sit still and be quiet in church. He knows he's not supposed to be noisy, but he hits his toys on the pew and sometimes talks out loud. Should I spank him for being disruptive?
Your question reveals a rather poor understanding of the nature of toddlers. Most two-year-olds can no more fold their hands and sit still in church and listen to the sermon than they could swim the Atlantic Ocean. They squirm and churn and burn because they *must*. You just can't hold a toddler down. All their waking hours are spent in activity, and that's normal for this stage of development. So I do not recommend that your child be punished for this behavior. I think he should be left in the church nursery where he can shake the foundations without

disturbing the worship service. If there is no nursery, I suggest, if it is possible from a financial point of view, that he be left at home with a sitter until he is at least three years of age.[8]

At what age could you expect a child to sit quietly in church?

The ability to sit quietly in church is a gradually developing example of self-control. He will learn it in small increments during the first few years of his life. I would expect that perhaps by four years of age he should be able to control his activity and sit in church without making any loud disturbance, even if he is drawing or coloring or looking at books. By the time he is five he should be ready to sit through the service without dropping things, waving his arms around, etc. But even at that age, punishment for noise is inappropriate except in instances of deliberate and willful defiance.[9]

I have to spank my toddler most frequently for touching the china and expensive trinkets which decorate our home. How can I make her leave these breakable things alone?

I caution parents not to punish toddlers for behavior which is natural and necessary to learning and development. Exploration of their environment, for example, is of great importance to intellectual stimulation. You and I as adults will look at a crystal trinket and obtain whatever information we seek from that visual inspection. A toddler, however, will expose it to all of her senses. She will pick it up, taste it, smell it, wave it in the air, pound it on the wall, throw it across the room, and listen to the pretty sound that it makes when shattering. By that process she learns a bit about gravity, rough versus smooth surfaces, the brittle nature of glass, and some startling things about mother's anger.

I am not suggesting that your child be allowed to destroy your home and all of its contents. Neither is it right to expect her to keep her hands to herself. Parents should remove those items that are fragile or particularly dangerous, and then strew the child's path with fascinating objects of all types. Permit her to explore everything possible and do not ever punish her for touching something that she *did not know was off limits*, regardless of its value. With respect to dangerous items, such as electric plugs and stoves, as well as a few untouchable objects, such as the knobs on the television set, it is possible and necessary to teach and enforce the command, "Don't touch!" After making it clear what is expected, a thump on the fingers or slap on the hands will usually discourage repeat episodes.[10]

When, then, should the toddler be subjected to mild punishment?

When he openly defies his parents' spoken commands! If he runs the other way when called—if he slams his milk on the floor—if he screams and throws a tantrum at bedtime—if he hits his friends—these are the forms of unacceptable behavior which should be discouraged. Even in these situations, however, all-out spankings are not often required to eliminate the response. A firm thump or a rap on the fingers will convey the same message just as convincingly. Spankings should be reserved for moments of greatest antagonism during later years.

I feel it is important to stress this point: the toddler years are critical to the child's future attitude toward authority. He should be patiently taught to obey without being expected to behave like an adult.[11]

My three-year-old daughter, Nancy, plays unpleasant games with me in grocery stores. She runs when I call her and makes demands for candy and gum and cupcakes. When I refuse, she throws the most embarrassing temper tantrums you can imagine. I don't want to punish her in front of all those people, and she knows it. What should I do?

If there are sanctuaries where the usual rules and restrictions do not apply, then your children will behave differently in those protected zones than elsewhere. I would suggest that you have a talk with Nancy on the next trip to the market. Tell her exactly what you expect, and make it clear that you mean business. Then when the same behavior occurs, take her to the car or behind the building and do what you would have done at home. She'll get the message.

In the absence of this kind of away-from-home parental leadership, some children become extremely obnoxious and defiant, especially in public places. Perhaps the best example was a ten-year-old boy named Robert, who was a patient of my good friend Dr. William Slonecker. Dr. Slonecker said his pediatric staff dreaded the days when Robert was scheduled for an office visit. He literally attacked the clinic, grabbing instruments and files and telephones. His passive mother could do little more than shake her head in bewilderment.

During one physical examination, Dr. Slonecker observed severe cavities in Robert's teeth and knew that the boy must be referred to a local dentist. But who would be given the honor? A referral like Robert could mean the end of a professional friendship. Dr. Slonecker eventually decided to send him to an older dentist who reportedly understood children. The confrontation that followed now stands as one of the classic moments in the history of human conflict.

Robert arrived in the dentist's office, prepared for battle.

"Get into the chair, young man," said the doctor.

"No chance!" replied the boy.

"Son, I told you to climb onto the chair, and that's what I intend for you to do," said the dentist.

Robert stared at his opponent for a moment and then replied, "If you make me get in that chair, I will take off all my clothes."

The dentist calmly said, "Son, take 'em off."

The boy forthwith removed his shirt, undershirt, shoes and socks, and then looked up in defiance.

"All right, son," said the dentist. "Now get on the chair."

"You didn't hear me," sputtered Robert. "I said if you make me get on that chair I will take off *all* my clothes."

"Son, take 'em off," replied the man.

Robert proceeded to remove his pants and shorts, finally standing totally naked before the dentist and his assistant.

"Now, son, get into the chair," said the doctor.

Robert did as he was told, and sat cooperatively through the entire procedure. When the cavities were drilled and filled, he was instructed to step down from the chair.

"Give me my clothes now," said the boy.

"I'm sorry," replied the dentist. "Tell your mother that we're going to keep your clothes tonight. She can pick them up tomorrow."

Can you comprehend the shock Robert's mother received when the door to the waiting room opened, and there stood her pink son, as naked as the day he was born? The room was filled with patients, but Robert and his mom walked past them and into the hall. They went down a public elevator and into the parking lot, ignoring the snickers of onlookers.

The next day, Robert's mother returned to retrieve his clothes, and asked to have a word with the dentist. However, she did not come to protest. These were her sentiments: "You don't know how much I appreciate what happened here yesterday. You see, Robert has been blackmailing me about his clothes for years. Whenever we are in a public place, such as a grocery store, he makes unreasonable demands of me. If I don't immediately buy him what he wants, he threatens to take off all his clothes. You are the first person who has called his bluff, doctor, and the impact on Robert has been incredible!"[12]

I know you recommend that spanking should be relatively infrequent during toddler years. What is another disciplinary technique for a child this age who has been disobedient?

One possible approach is to require the boy or girl to sit in a chair and think about what he has done. Most children of this age are bursting with energy and absolutely hate to spend ten dull minutes with their wiggly posteriors glued to a chair. To some individuals, this form of punishment can be even more effective than a spanking, and is remembered longer.[13]

What can I do if Johnny, my three-year-old, refuses to stay in bed at night? He climbs right out while I'm standing there telling him to stay put!

The parent who cannot require a toddler to stay on a chair or in his bed is not yet in command of the child. There is no better time than now to change the relationship.

I would suggest that the youngster be placed in bed and given a little speech, such as, "Johnny, this time Mommie means business. Are you listening to me? *Do not* get out of this bed. Do you understand me?" Then when Johnny's feet touch the floor, give him one swat on the legs with a small switch. Put the switch on his dresser where he can see it, and promise him one more stroke if he gets up again. Walk confidently out of the room without further comment. If he rebounds again, fulfill your promise and offer the same warning if he doesn't stay in bed. Repeat the episode until Johnny acknowledges that you are the boss. Then hug him, tell him you love him, and remind him how important it is for him to get his rest so that he won't be sick, etc. Your purpose in this painful exercise (painful for both parties) is not only to keep li'l John in bed, but to confirm your leadership in his mind. It is my opinion that too many American parents lack the courage to win this kind of confrontation and are off-balance and defensive ever after. Dr. Benjamin Spock wrote in 1974, "Inability to be firm is, to my mind, the commonest problem of parents in America today." I agree.[14]

We have an adopted child who came to us when he was two years old. He was so abused during those first couple of years that my husband and I cannot let ourselves punish him, even when he deserves it. We also feel we don't have the right to discipline him, since we are not his real parents. Are we doing right?

I'm afraid you are making a mistake commonly committed by the parents of adopted children. They pity their youngsters too much to control them. They feel that life has already been too harsh with the little ones, and they must not make things worse by disciplining them. As you indicated, there is often the feeling that they do not have the right to make demands on their adopted children. These guilt-laden attitudes can lead to unfortunate consequences. Transplanted children have the same needs for guidance and discipline as those remaining with their biological parents. One of the surest ways to make a child feel insecure is to treat him as though he is different— unusual—brittle. If the parents view him as an unfortunate waif to be shielded, he will see himself that way too.

Parents of sick and deformed children are also likely to find discipline harder to implement. A child with a withered arm or some nonfatal illness can become a little terror, simply because the usual behavioral boundaries are not established by his parents. It must be remembered that the need to be controlled and governed is almost universal in childhood; this need is not eliminated by other problems and difficulties in life. In some cases, the desire for boundaries is maximized by other troubles, for it is through loving control that parents express personal worth to a child.[15]

SECTION 7

UNDER-STANDING THE ROLE OF DISCIPLINE

Why is there so much confusion on the subject of discipline today? Is it really that difficult to raise our children properly?

Parents are confused because they have been taught an illogical, unworkable approach to child management by many professionals who ought to know better. Child development authorities have muddied the water with permissive philosophies which contradict the very nature of children. Let me cite an example. *Growing Pains* is a question-and-answer book for parents, published by the American Academy of Pediatrics (a division of the American Medical Association). The following question written by a parent is quoted in the book, along with the answer provided by the pediatrician.

CHILD SLAMS DOOR IN PARENT'S FACE

Q. What does one do when an angry child slams a door in one's face?

A. Step back. Then do nothing until you have reason to believe that the child's anger has cooled off. Trying to reason with an angry person is like hitting your head against a stone wall.

When the child is in a good mood, explain to him how dangerous door-slamming can be. Go so far as to give him a description of how a person can lose a finger from a slammed door. Several talks of this sort are generally enough to cure a door-slammer.

How inadequate is this reply, from my point of view. The writer failed to recognize that the door-slamming behavior was *not* the real issue in this situation. To the contrary, the child was demonstrating his defiance of parental authority, and for *that* he should have been held accountable. Instead, the parent is told to wait until the child is in a good mood (which could be next Thursday), and then talk about the dangers of door-slamming. It seems clear that the child was begging his mom to accept his challenge, but she was in the other room counting to ten and keeping cool. And let's all wish her lots of luck on the next encounter.

As I've stated, the great givers of parental advice have failed to offer a course of action to be applied in response to willful defiance. In the situation described above, for example, what is Mom supposed to do until Junior cools off? What if he is breaking furniture and writing on the back of that slammed door? What if he calls her dirty names and whacks his little sister across the mouth? You see, the *only* tool given to Mom by the writer, above, is postponed *reason*. And as every mother knows, reason is practically worthless in response to anger and disrespect.

Nature has provided a wonderfully padded place for use in moments of haughty defiance, and I wish the disciplinary "experts" were less confused as to its proper purpose.[1]

Permissiveness is a relative term. Please describe its meaning to you.

When I use the term permissiveness, I refer to the absence of effective parental authority, resulting in the lack of boundaries for the child. This word represents childish disrespect, defiance, and the general confusion that occurs in the absence of adult leadership.[2]

Do you think parents are now beginning to value discipline more? Is the day of permissiveness over?

Parents who tried extreme permissiveness have seen its failure, for the most part. Unfortunately, those parents will soon be grandparents, and the world will profit little from their experience. What worries me most is the kind of discipline that will be exercised by the generation now reaching young adulthood. Many of these new parents have never seen good discipline exercised. They have had no model. Besides, in many cases they have severed themselves from the best source of information, avowing that anyone over thirty is to be mistrusted. It will be interesting to see what develops from this blind date between mom and baby.[3]

Is it accurate to say that an undisciplined preschooler will continue to challenge his parents during the latter years of childhood?

It often occurs that way. When a parent loses the early confrontations with the child, the later conflicts become harder to win. The parent who never wins, who is too weak or too tired or too busy to win, is making a costly mistake that will usually come back to haunt him during the child's adolescence. If you can't make a five-year-old pick up his toys, it is unlikely that you will exercise any impressive degree of control during his adolescence, the most defiant time of life. It is important to understand that adolescence is a condensation or composite of all the training and behavior that has gone before. Any unsettled matter in the first twelve years is likely to fester and erupt during adolescence. Therefore, the proper time to begin disarming the teenage time-bomb is twelve years before it arrives.[4]

My first year as a teacher was a disaster. I loved the students as though they were my own children, but they totally rejected that affection. I simply couldn't control them. Since then, I've learned that children can't accept love until they have tested the strength and courage of their teachers. Why do you think this is true?

I don't know. But every competent teacher will verify the fact that respect for authority must precede the acceptance of love. Those teachers who try to spread love in September and discipline the following January are destined for trouble. It won't work. (That's why I have recommended—half seriously—that teachers not smile 'til Thanksgiving!)

Perhaps the most frustrating experience of my professional career occurred when I was asked to speak to a group of college students who were majoring in education. The year was 1971, when permissive philosophies were rampant . . . especially on college campuses. Most of these men and women were in their final year of preparation, and would soon be teaching in their own classrooms. The distress that I felt came from my inability to convince these idealistic young people of the principle you have observed. They really believed that they could pour out love to their students and be granted instant respect from these rebels who had been at war with everyone. I felt empathy for the new teachers who would soon find themselves in the jungles of inner city schools, alone and afraid. They were bound to get their "love" thrown back in their startled faces, just as you did. *Students simply cannot accept a teacher's love until they know that the giver is worthy of their respect.*

You might be interested to know that I have made the same observation in other areas of life, including man's relationship with God. Remember that He revealed His majesty and wrath and justice through the Old Testament before we were permitted to observe Jesus' incomparable love in the New Testament. It would appear that respect must precede loving relationships in all areas of life.[5]

Some parents feel guilty about demanding respect from their children, because it could be an underhanded way of making themselves feel powerful and important. What do you think?

I disagree. It is most important that a child respect his parents, because that relationship provides the basis for his attitude toward all other people. His view of parental authority becomes the cornerstone for his later outlook on school authority, police and law, the people with whom he will eventually live and work, and for society in general.

Another equally important reason for maintaining parental respect is that if you want your child to accept your values when he reaches his teen years, then you must be worthy of his respect during his younger days.

When a child can successfully defy his parents during his first fifteen years, laughing in their faces and stubbornly flouting their authority, he develops a natural contempt for them. "Stupid old Mom and Dad! I've got them wound around my little finger. Sure they love me, but I really think they're afraid of me." A child may not utter these words, but he feels them each time he outsmarts his adult companions and wins the confrontations and battles. Later he is likely to demonstrate his disrespect in a more open matter. His parents are not deserving of his respect, and he does not want to identify with anything they represent. He rejects every vestige of their philosophy.

This factor is important for Christian parents who wish to sell their concept of God to their children. They must first sell themselves. If they are not worthy of respect, then neither is their religion or their morals, or their government, or their country, or any of their values. This becomes the "generation gap" at its most basic level. The chasm does not develop from a failure to communicate; we're speaking approximately the same language. Mark Twain once said about the Bible, "It's not the things I don't understand that bother me; it's the things I do!" Likewise, our difficulties between generations result more from what we *do* understand in our communication than in our confusion with words. The conflict between generations occurs because of a breakdown in mutual respect, and it bears many painful consequences.[6]

You place great stress on the child being taught to respect the authority of the parents. But does that coin have two sides? Don't parents have an equal responsibility to show respect for their children?

They certainly do! A mother cannot require her child to treat her with dignity if she will not do the same for him. She should be gentle with his ego, never belittling him or embarrassing him in front of his friends. Punishment should be administered away from the curious eyes of gloating onlookers. The child should not be laughed at unmercifully. His strong feelings and requests, even if foolish, should be given an honest appraisal. He should feel that his parents "really *do* care about me." Self-esteem is the most fragile attribute in human nature; it can be damaged by very minor incidents and its reconstruction is often difficult to engineer. A father who is sarcastic and biting in his criticism of children cannot expect to receive genuine respect in return. His offspring might fear him enough to conceal their contempt, but revenge will often erupt in late adolescence.[7]

What goes through the mind of a child when he is openly defying the wishes of his parent?

Children are usually aware of the contest of wills between generations, and that is precisely why the parental response is so important. When a child behaves in ways that are disrespectful or harmful to himself or others, his hidden purpose is often to verify the stability of the boundaries. This testing has much the same function as a policeman who turns doorknobs at places of business after dark. Though he tries to open doors, he hopes they are locked and secure. Likewise, a child who assaults the loving authority of his parents is greatly reassured when their leadership holds firm and confident. He finds his greatest security in a structured environment where the rights of other people (and his own) are protected by definite boundaries.[8]

Could you explain further why *security* for the child is related to parental discipline and structure? It just doesn't add up for me. I guess I've been influenced by the psychologists and writers who stress the importance of children growing up in an atmosphere of freedom and democracy in the home.

After working with children for twenty-one years, I couldn't be more convinced that they draw confidence from knowing where their boundaries are and who intends to enforce them. Perhaps an illustration will make this more clear. Imagine yourself driving a car over the Royal Gorge in Colorado. The bridge is suspended hundreds of feet above the canyon floor, and as a first-time traveler, you are tense as you drive across. (I knew one little fellow who was so awed by the view over the side of the bridge that he said, "Wow, Daddy. If you fell off of here it'd kill you constantly!") Now suppose that there were no guardrails on the side of the bridge; where would you steer the car? Right down the middle of the road! Even though you don't plan to hit those protective walls along the side, you feel more secure just knowing they are there.

The analogy to children has been demonstrated empirically. During the early days of the progressive education movement, one enthusiastic theorist decided to take down the chain-link fence that surrounded the nursery school yard. He thought the children would feel more freedom of movement without that visible barrier surrounding them. When the fence was removed, however, the boys and girls huddled near the center of the play yard. Not only did they not wander away, they didn't even venture to the edge of the grounds.

There is a security in defined limits. When the home atmosphere is as it should be, the child lives in utter safety. He never gets in trouble unless he deliberately asks for it, and as long as he stays within the limits, there is mirth and freedom and acceptance. If this is what is meant by "democracy" in the home, then I favor it. If it means the absence of boundaries, or that each child sets his own boundaries, then I'm inalterably opposed to it.[9]

Everyone tells me that children love justice and law and order. If that's true, why doesn't my little son respond better to me when I talk reasonably with him about his misbehavior? Why do I have to resort to some form of punishment to make him listen to me?

The answer is found in a curious value system of children which respects strength and courage (when combined with love). What better explanation can be given for the popularity of the mythical Superman and Captain Marvel and Wonder Woman in the folklore of children? Why else do children proclaim, "My dad can beat up your dad"? (One child replied to that statement, "That's nothing, my *mom* can beat up my dad, too!")

You see, boys and girls care about the issue of "who's toughest." Whenever a youngster moves into a new neighborhood or a new school district, he usually has to fight (either verbally or physically) to establish himself in the hierarchy of strength. Anyone who understands children knows that there is a "top dog" in every group, and there is a poor little defeated pup at the bottom of the heap. And every child between those extremes knows where he stands in relation to the others.

This respect for strength and courage also makes children want to know how "tough" their leaders are. They will occasionally disobey parental instructions for the precise purpose of testing the determination of those in charge. Thus, whether you are a parent or grandparent or Boy Scout leader or bus driver or Brownie leader or a schoolteacher, I can guarantee that sooner or later, one of the children under your authority will clench his little fist and challenge your leadership.

This defiant game, called "Challenge the Chief," can be played with surprising skill by very young children. A father told me of taking his three-year-old daughter to a basketball game. The child was, of course, interested in everything in the gym except the athletic contest. The father permitted her to roam free and climb on the bleachers, but he set up definite limits regarding how far she could stray. He took her by the hand and walked with her to a stripe painted on the gym floor. "You can play all around the building, Janie, but don't go past this line," he instructed her. He had no sooner returned to his seat than the toddler scurried in the direction of the forbidden territory. She stopped at the border for a moment, then flashed a grin over her shoulder to her father, and deliberately placed one foot over the line as if to say, "Whacha gonna do about it?" Virtually every parent the world over has been asked the same question at one time or another.

The entire human race is afflicted with this tendency toward willful defiance. God told Adam and Eve that they could eat anything in the Garden of Eden except the forbidden fruit. Yet they challenged the authority of the Almighty by deliberately disobeying His commandment. Perhaps this tendency toward self-will is the essence of "original sin" which has infiltrated the human family. It certainly explains why I place such stress on the proper response to willful defiance during childhood, for that rebellion can plant the seeds of personal disaster. The thorny weed which it produces may grow into a tangled briar patch during the troubled days of adolescence.

When a parent refuses to accept his child's defiant challenge, something changes in their relationship. The youngster begins to look at his mother and father with disrespect; they are unworthy of his allegiance. More important, he wonders why they would let him do such harmful things if they really loved him. The ultimate paradox of childhood is that boys and girls want to be led by their parents, but insist that their mothers and fathers earn the right to lead them.[10]

Isn't it our goal to produce children with *self*-discipline and *self*-reliance? If so, how does your approach to *external* discipline by parents get translated into internal control?
You've asked a provocative question, but one that reveals a misunderstanding of children, I believe. There are many authorities who suggest that parents not discipline their children for the reason implied by your question: they want

their kids to discipline themselves. But since young people lack the maturity to generate that self-control, they stumble through childhood without experiencing *either* internal or external discipline. Thus, they enter adult life having never completed an unpleasant assignment, or accepted an order that they disliked, or yielded to the leadership of their elders. Can we expect such a person to exercise self-discipline in young adulthood? I think not. He doesn't even know the meaning of the word.

My concept is that parents should introduce their child to discipline and self-control by the use of external influences when he is young. By being required to behave responsibly, he gains valuable experience in controlling his own impulses and resources. Then as he grows into the teen years, the transfer of responsibility is made year by year from the shoulders of the parent directly to the child. He is no longer forced to do what he has learned during earlier years. To illustrate, a child should be *required* to keep his room relatively neat when he is young. Then somewhere during the midteens, his own self-discipline should take over and provide the motivation to continue the task. If it does not, the parent should close the door and let him live in a dump, if necessary.[11]

I have been hearing about "Parent Effectiveness Training" classes offered in various parts of the country. What do you think of them?

Dr. Thomas Gordon is the creator of this program, which has become very widespread. There are more than 8,000 P. E. T. classes in operation throughout the country. These sessions offer some worthwhile suggestions in the area of listening skills, in the use of parent-child negotiation, and in the cultivation of parental tolerance.

Nevertheless, it is my view that the great flaws in Tom Gordon's philosophy far outweigh the benefits. They are: (1) his failure to understand the proper role of authority in the home; (2) his humanistic viewpoint which teaches that children are born innately "good," and then learn to do wrong; (3) his tendency to weaken parental resolve to instill spiritual principles systematically during a child's "teachable" years.[12]

(For a complete discussion of the Parent Effectiveness Training program, see *The Strong-Willed Child*, Chapter 7.)

I would like to compare your approach to discipline with that of Dr. Tom Gordon. He often cites an illustration of a child who puts his feet on an expensive item of living room furniture. His parents become irritated at this gesture and order him to take his dirty shoes from the chair or table. Gordon then shows how much more politely those parents would have handled the same indiscretion if the offender had been an adult guest. They might have cautiously asked him to remove his shoes, but would certainly not have felt it necessary to discipline or criticize the visitor. Dr. Gordon then asks, "Aren't children people, too? Why don't we treat them with the same respect that we do our adult friends?" Would you comment on this example?

I have heard Dr. Gordon relate the same illustration and feel that it contains both truth and distortion. If his point is that we need to exercise greater kindness and respect in dealing with our children, then I certainly agree. However, to equate children with adult visitors in the home is an error in reasoning. I do not bear *any* responsibility for teaching proper manners and courtesy to my guests; I certainly do have that obligation on behalf of my children. Furthermore, the illustration implies that children and adults think and act identically, and have the same needs. They don't. A child often behaves offensively for the precise purpose of testing the courage of his parents. He wants them to establish firm boundaries. By contrast, a guest who puts his feet on a coffee table is more likely to be acting through ignorance or insensitivity.

More important, this illustration cleverly redefines the traditional parental relationship with children. Instead of bearing direct responsibility for training and teaching and leading them, Mom and Dad have become cautious co-equals who can only hope their independent little "guests" will gradually get the message.

No, our children are not casual guests in our home. They have been loaned to us temporarily for the purpose of loving them and instilling a foundation of values on which their future lives will be built. And we will be accountable through eternity for the way we discharge that responsibility.[13]

Dr. Gordon and others condemn the use of parental "power" which he defines as being synonymous with parental authority. Do you also equate the meaning of these two words?

No, and that is a major distinction between Dr. Gordon's view of proper parenting and my own. It would appear from his writings that he views all authority as a form of unethical oppression. In my opinion, the two concepts are as different as love and hate. Parental power can be defined as a hostile form of manipulation in order to satisfy selfish adult purposes. As such, it disregards the best interests of the little child on whom it tramples, and produces a relationship of fear and intimidation. Drill instructors in the Marine Corps have been known to depend on this form of power to indoctrinate their beleaguered recruits.

Proper authority, by contrast, is defined as loving *leadership*. Without decision-makers and others who agree to follow, there is inevitable chaos and confusion and disorder in human relationships. Loving authority is the glue that holds social orders together, and it is absolutely necessary for the healthy functioning of a family.

There are times when I say to my child, "Ryan, you are tired because you were up too late last night. I want you to brush your teeth right now and put on your pajamas." My words may sound like a suggestion, but Ryan would be wise to remember who's making it. If that is parental power, according to Dr. Gordon's definition, then so be it. I do not always have time to negotiate, nor do I feel obligated in every instance to struggle for compromise. I have the *authority* to do what I think is in Ryan's best interest, and there are times when I expect him not to negotiate, but to *obey*. And, of critical importance, his learning to yield to my loving leadership is excellent training for his later submission to the loving authority of God. This is very different from the use of vicious and hostile power, resulting from the fact that I outweigh him.[14]

How about Gordon's suggested use of "I" messages versus "you" messages?

There is substantial truth in the basic idea. "I" messages can request change or improvement without being offensive: "Diane, it embarrasses me when our neighbors see your messy room. I wish you would straighten it." By contrast, "you" messages often attack the personhood of the recipient and put him on the defensive: "Why don't you keep your stuff picked up? So help me, Diane, you get sloppier and more irresponsible every day!" I agree with Dr. Gordon that the first method of communicating is usually superior to the second, and there is wisdom in his recommendation.

However, let's suppose I have taken my four-year-old son, Dale, to the market where he breaks all known rules. He throws a temper tantrum because I won't buy him a balloon, and he hits the daughter of another customer, and grabs a handful of gum at the checkout stand. When I get darlin' Dale outside the store there is little doubt that he is going to hear a few "you" messages—such as, "When *you* get home, young man, *you* are going to have *your* bottom tanned!"

From my perspective, again, there are few occasions in the life of a parent when he speaks not as an equal or a comrade or a pal, but as an *authority.* And in those circumstances, an occasional "you" message will fit the circumstances better than an expression of personal frustration by the parent. [15]

Dr. Gordon said parents cannot know what is in the best interest of their children. Do you claim to make weighty decisions on behalf of your kids with unshakable confidence? How do you know that what you're doing will ultimately be healthy for them?
It is certain that I will make mistakes and errors as a parent. My human frailties are impossible to hide and my children occasionally fall victim to those imperfections. But I cannot abandon my responsibilities to provide leadership simply because I lack infinite wisdom and insight. Besides, I do have more experience and a better perspective on which to base those decisions than my children possess at this time. I've *been* where they're going.

Perhaps a crude example would be illustrative. My daughter has a pet hamster (uncreatively named Hammy) who has a passion for freedom. He spends a portion of every night gnawing on the metal bars of his cage and forcing his head through the trap door. Recently I sat watching Hammy busily trying to escape. But I was not the only one observing the furry little creature. Sitting in the shadows a few feet away was old Sigmund, our dachshund. His erect ears, squinted eyes, and panting tongue betrayed his sinister thoughts. Siggie was thinking, "Come on, baby, break through to freedom! Bite those bars, Hambone, and I'll give you a thrill like you've never experienced!"

How interesting, I thought, that the hamster's greatest desire would bring him instant and violent death if he should be so unfortunate to achieve it. Hammy simply lacked the perspective to realize the folly of his wishes. The application to human experience was too striking to be missed and I shook my head silently as the animal drama spoke to me. There are occasions when the longings and desires of our children would be harmful or disastrous if granted. They would choose midnight bedtime hours and no schoolwork and endless cartoons on television and chocolate sundaes by the dozen. And in later years, they might not see the harm of drug abuse and premarital sex and a life of uninterrupted fun and games. Like Hammy, they lack the "perspective" to observe the dangers which lurk in the shadows. Alas, many young people are "devoured" before they even know that they have made a fatal mistake.

Then my thoughts meandered a bit farther to my own relationship with God and the requests I submit to Him in personal prayer. I wondered how many times I had asked Him to open the door on my "cage," not appreciating the security it was providing. I resolved to accept His negative answers with greater submission in the future.

Returning to the question, let me repeat that my decisions on behalf of my children do not reflect infinite wisdom. They do, however, emanate from love and an intense desire to do the best I can. Beyond that, the ultimate outcome is committed to God virtually every day of my life.[16]

My mother and father were harsh disciplinarians when I was a child, and I was afraid of them both. My cousin, on the other hand, was raised in a home with very few rules. She was a spoiled brat then and is still selfish today. Would you compare these two approaches to child rearing—the authoritarian and the permissive homes—and describe their effects on children?

They are equally harmful to children, in my view. On the side of harshness, a child suffers the humiliation of total domination. The atmosphere at home is icy and rigid, and he lives in constant fear of punishment. He is unable to make his own decisions and his personality is squelched beneath the hob-nailed boot of parental power. Lasting characteristics of dependency, hostility and even psychosis can emerge from this overbearing oppression. The opposite approach, ultimate permissiveness, is equally tragic. In this setting, the child is his own master from his earliest babyhood. He thinks the world revolves around his heady empire, and he often has utter contempt and disrespect for those closest to him. Anarchy and chaos reign in his home and his mother is often the most nervous, frustrated woman on her block. When the child is young, his mother is stranded at home because she is too embarrassed to take her little devil anywhere. He later finds it difficult to yield to outside symbols of authority, such as teachers, police, ministers or even God.

To repeat, both extremes of authority are disastrous for the well being of a child. There is safety only in the middle ground, which is sometimes difficult for parents to locate.[17]

You have said that your philosophy of discipline (and of family advice in general) was drawn from the Scriptures. On what references do you base your views, and especially your understanding of the will and the spirit?
The dual responsibility assigned to parents appears repeatedly in the Scriptures, but is addressed most clearly in two passages:

SHAPING THE WILL
He [the father] must have proper authority in his own household, and be able to control and command the respect of his children (1 Tim. 3:4, 5 Phillips).

PRESERVING THE SPIRIT
Children, the right thing for you to do is to obey your parents as those whom the Lord has set over you. The first commandment to contain a promise was: "Honour thy father and thy mother that it may be well with thee, and that thou mayest live long on the earth." *Fathers, don't over-correct your children or make it difficult for them to obey the commandment. Bring them up with Christian teaching in Christian discipline* (Eph. 6:1-4 Phillips, emphasis added).

It is significant that this second Scripture instructs children to obey their parents but is followed immediately by admonitions to fathers regarding the limits of discipline. We see an identical pattern in Colossians 3:20, 21:

> Children, obey your parents in everything, for this pleases
> the Lord. Fathers, do not provoke your children, lest they
> become discouraged (RSV).

Another favorite Scripture of mine makes it clear that a
parent's relationship with his child should be modeled after
God's relationship with man. In its ultimate beauty, that
interaction is characterized by abundant love—a love
unparalleled in tenderness and mercy. This same love leads the
benevolent father to guide, correct—and even bring some pain
to the child when it is necessary for his eventual good.

> "My son, do not regard lightly the discipline of the Lord,
> nor lose courage when you are punished by him. For the
> Lord disciplines him whom he loves [Note: Discipline and
> love work hand in hand; one being a function of the other],
> and chastises every son whom he receives." It is for
> discipline that you have to endure. God is treating you as
> sons; for what son is there whom his father does not
> discipline? If you are left without discipline, in which all
> have participated, then you are illegitimate children and
> not sons. Besides this, we have had earthly fathers to
> discipline us and we respected them. [Note: the
> relationship between discipline and respect was recognized
> more than 2,000 years ago.] For the moment all discipline
> seems painful rather than pleasant; later it yields the
> peaceful fruit of righteousness to those who have been
> trained by it (Heb. 12:5-9, 11 RSV).

The Book of Proverbs is replete with similar instructions to
parents regarding the importance of authority and discipline.
Let me quote a few examples:

> Foolishness is bound in the heart of a child; but the rod of
> correction shall drive it far from him (Prov. 22:15 KJV).
> Withhold not correction from the child: for if thou beatest
> him with the rod, he shall not die. Thou shalt beat him with
> the rod, and shalt deliver his soul from hell (Prov. 23:13, 14
> KJV).
> He that spareth his rod hateth his son: but he that loveth
> him chasteneth him betimes (Prov. 13:24 KJV).
> The rod and reproof give wisdom: but a child left to himself
> bringeth his mother to shame (Prov. 29:15 KJV).
> Correct thy son, and he shall give thee rest; yea, he shall
> give delight unto thy soul (Prov. 29:17 KJV).

Why is parental authority so vigorously supported through-out the Bible? Is it simply catering to the whims of oppressive, power-hungry adults, as some modern educators surmise? No, the leadership of parents plays a significant role in the development of a child! By learning to yield to the loving authority (leadership) of his parents, a child learns to submit to other forms of authority which will confront him later in life. The way he sees his parents' leadership sets the tone for his eventual relationships with his teachers, school principal, police, neighbors, and employers. These forms of authority are necessary to healthy human relationships. Without respect for leadership, there is anarchy, chaos, and confusion for everyone concerned. And ultimately, of course, respect of earthly authority teaches children to yield to the benevolent authority of God Himself.

On this and other relevant issues, the Bible offers a consistent foundation on which to build an effective philosophy of parent-child relationships. It is my belief that we have departed from the standard which was clearly outlined in both the Old and New Testaments, and that deviation is costing us a heavy toll in the form of social turmoil. Self-control, human kindness, respect, and peacefulness can again be manifest in America if we will return to this ultimate resource in our homes and schools.[18]

SECTION 8

THE "HOW TO" OF DISCIPLINE

Philosophically, I recognize the need to take charge of my kids. But that isn't enough to help me discipline properly. Give me a step by step set of instructions that will help me do the job correctly.

All right, let me outline six broad guidelines that I think you'll be able to apply. These principles represent the essence of my philosophy of discipline.

First: Define the boundaries before they are enforced. The most important step in any disciplinary procedure is to establish reasonable expectations and boundaries *in advance.* The child should know what is and what is not acceptable behavior *before* he is held responsible for those rules. This precondition will eliminate the overwhelming sense of injustice that a youngster feels when he is slapped or punished for his accidents, mistakes, and blunders. If you haven't defined it—don't enforce it!

Second: When defiantly challenged, respond with confident decisiveness. Once a child understands what is expected, he should then be held accountable for behaving accordingly. That sounds easy, but as we have seen, most children will assault the authority of their elders and challenge their right to lead. In a moment of rebellion, a little child will consider his parents' wishes and defiantly choose to disobey. Like a military general before a battle, he will calculate the potential risk, marshal his forces, and attack the enemy with guns blazing. When that nose-to-nose confrontation occurs between generations, it is *extremely* important for the adult to win decisively and confidently. The child has made it clear that he's looking for a fight, and his parents would be wise not to disappoint him! *Nothing* is more destructive to parental leadership than for a mother or father to disintegrate during that struggle. When the parent consistently loses those battles, resorting to tears and screaming and other evidence of frustration, some dramatic changes take place in the way they are "seen" by their children. Instead of being secure and confident leaders, they become spineless jellyfish who are unworthy of respect or allegiance.

Third: Distinguish between willful defiance and childish irresponsibility. A child should not be spanked for behavior that is not willfully defiant. When he forgets to feed the dog or make his bed or take out the trash—when he leaves your tennis racket outside in the rain or loses his bicycle—remember that these behaviors are typical of childhood. It is, more than likely, the mechanism by which an immature mind is protected from adult anxieties and pressures. Be gentle as you teach him to do better. If he fails to respond to your patient instruction, it then becomes appropriate to administer some well-defined consequences (he may have to work to pay for the item he abused or be deprived of its use, etc.). However, childish irresponsibility is very different from willful defiance, and should be handled more patiently.

Fourth: Reassure and teach after the confrontation is over. After a time of conflict during which the parent has demonstrated his right to lead (particularly if it resulted in tears for the child), the youngster between two and seven (or older) may want to be loved and reassured. By all means, open your arms and let him come! Hold him close and tell him of your love. Rock him gently and let him know, again, why he was punished and how he can avoid the trouble next time. This moment of communication builds love, fidelity, and family unity. And for the Christian family, it is extremely important to pray with the child at that time, admitting to God that we have *all* sinned and no one is perfect. Divine forgiveness is a marvelous experience, even for a very young child.

Fifth: Avoid impossible demands. Be absolutely sure that your child is *capable* of delivering what you require. Never punish him for wetting the bed involuntarily or for not becoming potty-trained by one year of age, or for doing poorly in school when he is incapable of academic success. These impossible demands put the child in an unresolvable conflict: there is no way out. That condition brings inevitable damage to human emotional apparatus.

Sixth: Let love be your guide! A relationship that is

characterized by genuine love and affection is likely to be a healthy one, even though some parental mistakes and errors are inevitable.[1]

I want to control and lead my strong-willed child properly, but I'm afraid I'll break his spirit and damage his emotions in some way. How can I deal with his misbehavior without hurting his self-concept?

I sense that you do not have a clear understanding of the difference between breaking the *spirit* of a child, and shaping his *will*. The human spirit, as I have defined it, relates to the self-esteem or the personal worth that a child feels. As such, it is exceedingly fragile at *all* ages and must be handled with care. You as a parent correctly assume that you can damage your child's spirit quite easily . . . by ridicule, disrespect, threats to withdraw love, and by verbal rejection. *Anything* that depreciates his self-esteem can be costly to his spirit.

However, while the spirit is brittle and must be treated gently, the will is made of steel. It is one of the few intellectual components which arrives full strength at the moment of birth. In a recent issue of *Psychology Today,* this heading described the research findings from a study of infancy: "A baby knows who he is before he has language to tell us so. He reaches deliberately for control of his environment, especially his parents." This scientific disclosure would bring no new revelation to the parents of a strong-willed infant. They have walked the floor with him in the wee small hours, listening to this tiny dictator as he made his wants and wishes abundantly clear.

Later, a defiant toddler can become so angry that he is capable of holding his breath until he loses consciousness. Anyone who has ever witnessed this full measure of willful defiance has been shocked by its power. One headstrong three-year-old recently refused to obey a direct command from her mother, saying, "You're just my *mommie,* you know!" Another mere mommie wrote me that she found herself in a similar confrontation with her three-year-old son over something that she wanted him to eat. He was so enraged by her insistence that he refused to eat or drink *anything* for two full days. He became weak and lethargic, but steadfastly held his ground. The mother was worried and guilt-ridden, as might be expected. Finally, in desperation, the father looked the child in the eyes and convinced him that he was going to receive a well deserved spanking if he didn't eat his dinner. With that maneuver, the contest was over. The toddler surrendered. He began to consume everything he could get his hands on, and virtually emptied the refrigerator.

Now tell me, please, why have so few child development authorities recognized this willful defiance? Why have they written so little about it? My guess is that the acknowledgment of childish imperfection would not fit neatly with the humanistic notion that little people are infused with sunshine and goodness, and merely "learn" the meaning of evil. To those who hold that rosy view I can only say, "Take another look!"

Returning to your question, your objective as a parent is to shape the will of your child while leaving his spirit intact.[2]

Then how can I do that? How can I shape my nine-year-old son's will without damaging his spirit?

It is accomplished by establishing reasonable boundaries and enforcing them with love, but by avoiding any implication that the child is unwanted, unnecessary, foolish, ugly, dumb, a burden, an embarrassment, or a disastrous mistake. Any accusation that assaults the worth of a child in this way can be costly, such as "You are so dumb!" Or, "Why can't you make decent grades in school like your sister?" Or, "You have been a pain in the neck ever since the day you were born!"

Rather, I would suggest that you respond decisively the next time your son behaves in a blatantly disruptive or defiant manner. There should be no screaming or derogatory accusations, although he should soon know that you mean what you say. He should probably be given a spanking and sent to bed an hour or two early. The following morning you should discuss the issue rationally, reassuring him of your continuing love, and then start over. Most rebellious preteenagers respond beautifully to this one-two punch of love and consistent discipline. It's an unbeatable combination.[3]

My wife and I have a strong-willed child who is incredibly difficult to handle. I honestly believe we are doing our job about as well as any parents would do, yet she still breaks the rules and challenges our authority. I guess I need

some encouragement. First, tell me if an especially strong-willed kid *can* be made to smile and give and work and cooperate. If so, *how* is that accomplished? And second, what is my daughter's future? I see trouble ahead, but don't know if that gloomy forecast is justified.

There is no question about it. A willful child such as yours can be difficult to control even when her parents handle her with great skill and dedication. It may take several years to bring her to a point of relative obedience and cooperation within the family unit. While this training program is in progress, it is important not to panic. Don't try to complete the transformation overnight. Treat your child with sincere love and dignity, but require her to follow your leadership. Choose carefully the matters which are worthy of confrontation, then accept her challenge on those issues and *win* decisively. Reward every positive, cooperative gesture she makes by offering your attention, affection, and verbal praise. Then take two aspirin and call me in the morning.

Concerning that second half of your question, I must admit that your daughter, *if not properly disciplined,* would be in a "high risk" category for antisocial behavior later in life. Such a child is more likely to challenge her teachers in school and question the values she has been taught and shake her fist in the faces of those who would lead her. I believe that youngster is more inclined toward sexual promiscuity and drug abuse and academic difficulties. This is not an inevitable prediction, of course, because the complexities of human personality make it impossible to forecast behavior with complete accuracy.

On the other hand, these dangers I have described are greatly minimized by parents who actively seek to shape the will of the children during the early years. That's why the future of your daughter is not a negative one. It is my belief that a strong-willed child like yours typically possesses more character and has greater potential for a productive life than her compliant counterpart. The key to reaching that potential is to gain a measure of control of the child's will and then, at the appropriate moment, transfer that control to the individual as she approaches the end of adolescence.

Sounds easy, doesn't it? It's a tough assignment, but God will help you accomplish it.[4]

You have described the nature of willfully defiant behavior and how parents should handle it. But does all unpleasant behavior result from this deliberate misbehavior?

No. Disobedience can be very different in origin from the "challenging" response I've been describing. A child's antagonism and negativism may emanate from frustration, disappointment, fatigue, illness, or rejection, and therefore must be interpreted as a warning signal to be heeded. Perhaps the toughest task in parenthood is to recognize the difference between these behavioral messages. A child's resistant behavior always contains a message to his parents which they must decode before responding.

For example, he may be saying, "I feel unloved now that I'm stuck with that yelling baby brother. Mom used to care for me; now nobody wants me. I hate everybody." When this kind of message underlies the rebellion, the parents should move quickly to pacify its cause. When a two-year-old screams and cries at bedtime, one must ascertain what he is communicating. If he is genuinely frightened by the blackness of his room, the appropriate response should be quite different than if he is merely protesting about having to go nighty-night. The art of good parenthood revolves around the interpretation of behavior.[5]

My six-year-old has suddenly become sassy and disrespectful in his manner at home. He told me to "buzz off" when I asked him to take out the trash, and he calls me names when he gets angry. I feel it is important to permit this emotional outlet, so I haven't suppressed it. Do you agree?

I couldn't disagree more strongly. Your son is aware of his sudden defiance, and he's waiting to see how far you will let him go. This kind of behavior, if unchecked, will continue to deteriorate day by day, producing a more profound disrespect with each encounter. If you don't discourage it, you can expect some wild experiences during the adolescent years to come. Thus, the behavior for which punishment is most necessary is that involving a direct assault on the leadership and personhood of the parent (or teacher), especially when the child obviously knows he shouldn't be acting that way.

With regard to the ventilation of anger, it is possible to let a child express his strongest feelings without being insulting or disrespectful. A tearful charge, "You weren't fair with me and you embarrassed me in front of my friends," should be accepted and responded to quietly and earnestly. But a parent should never permit a child to say, "You are so stupid and I wish you would leave me alone!" The first statement is a genuine expression of frustration based on a specific issue; the second is an attack on the dignity and authority of the parent. In my opinion, the latter is damaging to both generations and should be inhibited.[6]

How should I respond if my child says, "I hate you!" when he is angry?

If my child screamed his hatred at me *for the first time* in a moment of red-faced anger, I would probably wait until his passion had cooled and then convey this message in a loving and sincere manner: "Charlie, I know you were very upset earlier today when we had our disagreement, and I think we should talk about what you are feeling. *All* children get angry at their parents now and then, especially when they feel unfairly treated. I understand your frustration and I'm sorry we got into such a hassle. But that does not excuse you for saying, 'I hate you!' You'll learn that no matter how upset I become over something you've done, I'll *never* tell you that I hate you. And I can't permit you to talk that way to me. When people love each other, as you and I do, they don't want to hurt one another. It hurt me for you to say that you hated me, just as you would be hurt if I said something like that to you. You can, however, tell me what angers you, and I will listen carefully. If I am wrong, I will do my best to change the things you dislike. So I want you to understand that you are free to say *anything* you wish to me as always, even if your feelings are not very pleasant. But you will never be permitted to scream and call names and throw temper tantrums. If you behave in those childish ways, I will have to punish you. Is there anything you need to say to me now? (If not, then put your arms around my neck because I love you!)"

My purpose would be to permit the ventilation of negative feelings without encouraging violent, disrespectful, manipulative behavior.[7]

What is the most common error made by parents in disciplining their children?

In my opinion, it is the inappropriate use of *anger* in attempting to control boys and girls. There is no more ineffective method of influencing human beings (of all ages) than the use of irritation and anger. Nevertheless, *most* adults rely primarily on their own emotional response to secure the cooperation of children. One teacher said on a national television program, "I like being a professional educator, but I hate the daily task of teaching. My children are so unruly that I have to stay mad at them all the time just to control the classroom." How utterly frustrating to be required to be mean and angry as part of a routine assignment, year in and year out. Yet many teachers (and parents) know of no other way to lead children. Believe me, it is exhausting and it doesn't work!

Consider your *own* motivational system. Suppose you are driving your automobile home from work this evening, and you exceed the speed limit by forty miles per hour. Standing on the street corner is a lone policeman who has not been given the means to arrest you. He has no squad car or motorcycle; he wears no badge, carries no gun, and can write no tickets. All he is commissioned to do is stand on the curb and scream insults as you speed past. Would you slow down just because he shakes his fist in protest? Of course not! You might wave to him as you streak by. His anger would achieve little except to make him appear comical and foolish.

On the other hand, nothing influences the way Mr. Motorist drives more than occasionally seeing a black and white vehicle in hot pursuit with nineteen red lights flashing in the rear view mirror. When his car is brought to a stop, a dignified, courteous patrolman approaches the driver's window. He is six foot nine, has a voice like the Lone Ranger, and carries a sawed-off shotgun on each hip. "Sir," he says firmly but politely, "our radar unit indicates you were traveling sixty-five miles per hour in a twenty-five mile per hour zone. May I see your driver's license please?" He opens his leatherbound book of citations and leans toward you. He has revealed no hostility and offers no criticisms, yet you immediately go to pieces. You fumble nervously to locate the small document in your wallet. (The one with the horrible Polaroid picture.) Why are your hands moist and your mouth dry? Why is your heart thumping in your throat? Because the course of *action* that John Law is about to take is notoriously unpleasant. Alas, it is his *action* which dramatically affects your future driving habits.

Disciplinary *action* influences behavior; anger does not. As a matter of fact, I am convinced that adult anger produces a destructive kind of disrespect in the minds of our children. They perceive that our frustration is caused by our inability to control the situation. We represent justice to them, yet we're on the verge of tears as we flail the air with our hands and shout empty threats and warnings. Let me ask: Would *you* respect a superior court judge who behaved that emotionally in administering legal justice? Certainly not. This is why the judicial system is carefully controlled to appear objective, rational, and dignified.

I am not recommending that parents and teachers conceal their legitimate emotions from their children. I am not suggesting that we be like bland and unresponsive robots who hold everything inside. There are times when our boys and girls become insulting or disobedient and our irritation is entirely appropriate. In fact, it *should* be revealed, or else we appear phony and unreal. My point is merely that anger often becomes a *tool* used consciously for the purpose of influencing behavior. It is ineffective and can be damaging to the relationship between generations.[8]

What place should fear occupy in a child's attitude toward his mother or father?
There is a narrow difference between acceptable, healthy "awe" and destructive fear. A child should have a general apprehension about the consequences of defying his parent. By contrast, he should not lie awake at night worrying about parental harshness or hostility. Perhaps a crude example will illustrate the difference between these aspects of fear. A busy highway can be a dangerous place to take a walk. In fact, it would be suicidal to stroll down the fast lane of a freeway at 6:00 P.M. on any Friday. I would not be so foolish as to get my exercise in that manner because I have a healthy fear of fast-moving automobiles. As long as I don't behave ridiculously, I have no cause for alarm. I am unthreatened by this source of danger because it only reacts to my willful defiance. I want my child to view me with the same healthy regard. As long as he does not choose to challenge me, openly and willfully, he lives in total safety. He need not duck and flinch when I suddenly scratch my eyebrow. He should have no fear that I will ridicule him or treat him unkindly. He can enjoy complete security and safety—until

he chooses to defy me. Then he'll have to face the consequences. This concept of fear, which is better labeled "awe" or
"respect," is modeled after God's relationship with man. "Fear
of God is the beginning of wisdom," we are taught. He is a God of
justice, and at the same time, a God of infinite love and mercy.
These attributes are complementary, and should be represented
to a lesser degree in our homes.[9]

**I have an especially defiant five-year-old son, and I'm
doing my best to cope with the assignment of shaping his
will. But to be honest with you, I suffer from great
feelings of guilt and self-doubt most of the time. Lately, I
have been depressed over the constant tug of war I'm in
with this kid. Do other parents of strong-willed children
feel the same?**

Yes, many do. One of the problems is that parents have been
told by the "experts" that managing children is duck-soup for
those who do it right. That leaves them with intense
self-condemnation when things don't work that smoothly in
their homes. No one told them that parenthood would be this
difficult, and they blame themselves for the tension that arises.
They had planned to be such loving and effective parents,
reading fairy stories to their pajama-clad angels by the fireplace.
The difference between life as it is and life as it ought to be is a
frightening and distressing bit of reality.

I'm glad that you were able to verbalize your feelings of guilt
and depression. That is important. In response, let me give you
three assurances that will help you: (1) It *isn't* all your fault,
(2) It won't always be so difficult, (3) You're probably doing a
much better job than you think. Hang in there. Your
strong-willed child will someday be a stalwart, respectable,
hard-working citizen who's only source of depression will
emanate from conflict with his own strong-willed child.[10]

**I find it easier to say "no" to my children than to say
"yes," even when I don't feel strongly about the
permission they are seeking. I wonder why I automatically respond so negatively.**

It is easy to fall into the habit of saying "no" to our kids.

"No, you can't go outside."

"No, you can't have a cookie."

"No, you can't use the telephone."

"No, you can't spend the night with a friend."

We parents could have answered affirmatively to all of these requests, but chose almost automatically to respond in the negative. Why? Because we didn't take time to stop and think about the consequences; because the activity could cause us more work or strain; because there could be danger in the request; because our children ask for a thousand favors a day and we find it convenient to refuse them all.

While every child needs to be acquainted with denial of some of his more extravagant wishes, there is also a need for parents to consider each request on its own merit. There are so many necessary "no's" in life that we should say "yes" whenever we can.

Dr. Fitzhugh Dodson extended this idea in his book *How to Father*, saying that your child "needs time with you when you are not demanding anything from him, time when the two of you are mutually enjoying yourselves." I agree![11]

The children in our neighborhood are bratty with one another and disrespectful with adults. This upsets me, but I don't know what to do about it. I don't feel I have a right to discipline the children of my neighbors. How can I deal with this?

Parents in a neighborhood *must* learn to talk to each other about their kids, but that takes some doing! There is no quicker way to anger one mother than for another woman to criticize her precious cub. It is a delicate subject, indeed. That's why the typical neighborhood is like yours, providing little "feedback" to parents in regard to the behavior of their children. The kids know there are no lines of communication between adults and they take advantage of the barrier. What each block needs is a mother who has the courage to say, "I want to be told what my child does when he is beyond his own yard. If he is a brat with other children, I would like to know it. If he is disrespectful with adults, please mention it to me. I will not consider it tattling and I won't resent your coming to me. I hope I can share my insights regarding your children, too. None of our sons and daughters is perfect, and we'll know better how to teach them if we can talk openly to each other as adults."[12]

My husband and I are divorced, so I have to handle all the discipline of the children myself. How does this change the recommendations you've made about discipline in the home?

Not at all. The principles of good discipline remain the same, regardless of the family setting. The procedures do become somewhat harder for one parent, like yourself, to implement, since you have no one to support you when the children become defiant. You have to play the role of father *and* mother, which is not easily done. Nevertheless, children do not make allowances for your handicap. You must demand their respect or you will not receive it.[13]

My little girl is sometimes sugar-sweet, and other times she is unbearably irritating. How can I get her out of a bad mood when she has not really done anything to deserve punishment?

I would suggest that you take her in your arms and talk to her in this manner: "I don't know whether you've noticed it or not, but you have two 'personalities.' A personality is a way of acting and talking and behaving. One of your personalities is sweet and loving. No one could possibly be more lovable and happy when this personality is in control. It likes to work and look for ways to make the rest of the family happy. And all you have to do is press a little red button, 'ding,' and out comes the other personality. It is cranky and noisy and silly. It wants to fight with your brother and disobey your mom. It gets up grouchy in the morning and complains throughout the day.

"Now, I know that you can press the button for the neat personality or you can call up the mean one. Sometimes it takes some punishment to make you press the right button. If you keep on pressing the wrong one, like you have been today, then I'm going to make you uncomfortable, one way or the other. I'm tired of that cranky character and I want to see the grinny one. Can we make a deal?"

When discipline becomes a game, as in a conversation such as this, then you've achieved your purpose without conflict and animosity.[14]

Our six-year-old is extremely negative and disagreeable. He makes the entire family miserable and our attempts to discipline him have been ineffective. He just happens to have a sour disposition. How should we deal with him?

The objective with such a child is to define the needed changes and then reinforce those improvements when they occur. Unfortunately, attitudes are abstractions that a six-year-old may not fully understand, and you need a system that will clarify the "target" in his mind. Toward this end, I have developed an Attitude Chart (see illustration) which translates these subtle mannerisms into concrete mathematical terms. Please note: This system which follows would *not* be appropriate for the child who merely has a bad day, or displays temporary unpleasantness associated with illness, fatigue, or environmental circumstances. Rather, it is a remedial tool to help change persistently negative and disrespectful attitudes by making the child conscious of his problem.

The Attitude Chart should be prepared and then reproduced, since a separate sheet will be needed every day. Place an X in the appropriate square for each category, and then add the total points "earned" by bedtime. Although this nightly evaluation process has the appearance of being objective to a child, it is obvious that the parent can influence the outcome by considering it in advance (it's called cheating). Mom or Dad may want Junior to receive eighteen points on the first night, barely missing the punishment but realizing he must stretch the following day. I must emphasize, however, that the system will fail miserably if a naughty child does not receive the punishment he deserves, or if he hustles to improve but does not obtain the family fun he was promised. This approach is nothing more than a method of applying reward and punishment to attitudes in a way that children can understand and remember.

For the child who does not fully comprehend the concept of numbers, it might be helpful to plot the daily totals on a cumulative graph, such as the one provided below.

I don't expect everyone to appreciate this system or to apply it at home. In fact, parents of compliant, happy children will be puzzled as to why it would ever be needed. However, the mothers and fathers of sullen, ill-tempered children will comprehend more quickly. Take it or leave it, as the situation warrants.[15]

MY ATTITUDE CHART _____
DATE

	1 EXCELLENT	2 GOOD	3 OKAY	4 BAD	5 TERRIBLE
My Attitude Toward Mother					
My Attitude Toward Dad					
My Attitude Toward Sister					
My Attitude Toward Friends					
My Attitude Toward Work					
My Attitude At Bedtime					

TOTAL POINTS _____

CONSEQUENCES

6–9 POINTS	The family will do something fun together.
10–18 POINTS	Nothing happens, good or bad.
19–20 POINTS	I have to stay in my room for one hour.
21–22 POINTS	I get one swat with belt.
23 + POINTS	I get two swats with belt.

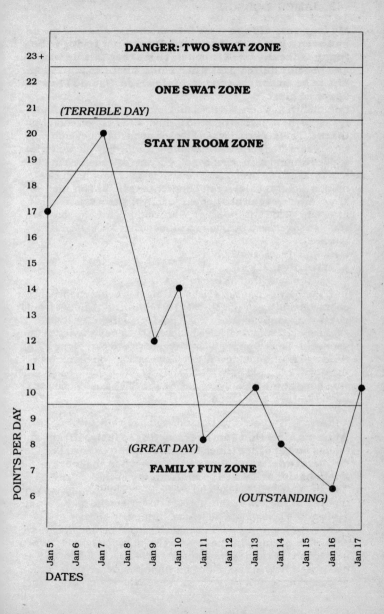

My four-year-old son came into the house and told me he had seen a lion in the backyard. He was not trying to be funny. He really tried to convince me that this lie was true and became quite upset when I didn't believe him. I want him to be an honest and truthful person. Should I have spanked him?

Definitely not. There is a *very* thin line between fantasy and reality in the mind of a preschool child, and he often confuses the two. This occurred when I took my son to Disneyland at three years of age. He was absolutely terrified by the wolf who stalked around with the three pigs. Ryan took one look at those sharp, jagged teeth and screamed in terror. I have a priceless motion picture of him scrambling for the safety of his mother's arms. After we returned home, I told Ryan there was a "very nice man" inside the wolf suit, who wouldn't hurt anyone. My son was so relieved by that news that he needed to hear it repeatedly.

He would say, "Dad?"

"What, Ryan?"

"Tell me 'bout that nice man!"

You see, Ryan was not able to distinguish between the fantasy character and a genuine threat to his health and safety. I would guess your son's lion story was a product of the same kind of confusion. He may well have believed that a lion was in the backyard. Thus, you would have been wise to play along with the game while making it perfectly clear that you didn't believe the story. You could have said, "My! My! A lion in the backyard. I sure hope he is a friendly old cat. Now, Billy, please wash your hands and come eat lunch."[16]

At times I feel that I am overreacting to insignificant issues and at other times I fail to respond to an act of deliberate defiance. How can I know when to ignore a misbehavior and when to confront my child?

The ability to "read" your child's thoughts and feelings is a skill that can be learned by the mother and father who take the time to study the behavior of their kids. Ultimately, the key to competent parenthood is in being able to get behind the eyes of your child, seeing what he sees and feeling what he feels. When he is lonely, he needs your company. When he is defiant, he needs your help in controlling his impulses. When he is afraid, he needs the security of your embrace. When he is curious, he needs your patient instruction. When he is happy, he needs to share his laughter and joy with those he loves.

Thus, the parent who learns to comprehend his child's feelings is in a position to respond appropriately and meet the needs that are apparent. And at this point, raising healthy children becomes a highly developed art, requiring the greatest wisdom, patience, devotion and love that God has given to us. The Apostle Paul called the Christian life a "reasonable service." We parents would do well to apply that same standard to the behavior of our children.

SPANKINGS: WHEN, HOW, AND WHY

As an advocate of spankings as a disciplinary tool, don't you worry about the possibility that you might be contributing to the incidence of child abuse in this country?

Yes, I do worry about that. One of my great frustrations in teaching parents has been the difficulty in conveying a *balanced* environment, wherein discipline is evident when necessary, but where it is matched by patience and respect and affection. Let it never be said that I favor the "slap 'em across the mouth" approach to authoritarianism. That hostile manner wounds the spirit and inflicts permanent scars on the psyche.

No subject distresses me more than the phenomenon of child abuse which is so prevalent in America today. There are children all across the country, even while I write, who are suffering untold miseries at the hands of their parents. Some of these pitiful little tots are brought to our hospital in every imaginable condition. They have been burned and bruised and broken and their little minds are permanently warped by the awful circumstances into which they were born.

Every professional who works with hurt children has to learn to cope with his own empathy. I have gained a measure of control over my own emotions; however, I have never been able to observe a battered child without feeling a literal agony within my chest. Diseased children suffer, of course, but most of them experience some degree of parental love which provides an emotional undergirding. But battered children suffer physically *and* emotionally. For them, no one cares. No one understands. There is no one to whom the longings can be expressed. They cannot escape. They cannot explain why they are hated. And many of them are too young to develop defense mechanisms or even call for help.

I dealt this spring with an eight-year-old girl who had been sexually assaulted repeatedly by her alcoholic father since she was fifteen months of age. What an immeasurable tragedy! Another child in Los Angeles was blinded by his mother, who destroyed his eyes with a razor blade. Can you imagine going through life knowing that your handicap resulted from a deliberate act by your own mother? Another small child in our city was pushed from a car on a crowded freeway and left clinging to the chain link divider for eight or nine hours. Another child's feet were held to a hot iron as punishment.

Just recently, a radio news summary broadcast through my office intercom told of finding a ten-year-old girl hanging by her heels in her parents' garage. These kinds of horror stories are all too familiar to those of us who work with children. In fact, it is highly probable that some youngster within a mile or two of your house is experiencing destructive abuse in one manner or another. Brian G. Fraser, attorney for the National Center for Prevention and Treatment of Child Abuse and Neglect, has written: "Child abuse . . . once thought to be primarily a problem of the poor and down-trodden . . . occurs in every segment of society and may be the country's leading cause of death in children."

The last thing on earth that I want to do is to provide a rationalization and justification for such parental oppression. Let me say it again: I don't believe in harsh, inflexible discipline, even when it is well intentioned. Children must be given room to breathe and grow and love. But there are also threatening circumstances at the permissive end of the spectrum, and many parents fall into one trap in an earnest attempt to avoid the other. These dual dangers were beautifully described by Marguerite and Willard Beecher, writing in their book *Parents on the Run:*[1]

> The adult-centered home of yesteryear made parents the masters and children their slaves. The child-centered home of today has made parents the slaves and children the masters. There is no true cooperation in any master-slave relationship, and therefore no democracy. Neither the restrictive-authoritative technique of rearing children nor the newer "anything goes" technique develop the genius within the individual, because neither trains him to be self-reliant . . . .

Children reared under arbitrary rules become either spineless automatons or bitter revolutionaries who waste their lives in conflict with those around them. But children who know no law higher than their own passing fancy become trapped by their own appetites. In either case, they are slaves. The former are enslaved by leaders on whom they depend to tell them what to do, and the latter are enslaved by the pawnbroker. Neither are [sic] capable of maintaining society on any decent basis. A lifetime of unhappiness may be avoided if the twig is bent so the tree will not incline in either of these mistaken directions.[2]

There is so much controversy now over the use of corporal punishment (spanking) that I would like to hear your rationale for the use of this approach. Specifically, what do you say to those who believe corporal punishment teaches children to hit and hurt others?
I debated a psychologist who held that view, on the Phil Donahue television show a few years ago. Let me quote from a comment attributed to Dr. John Valusek by *Parade Magazine.*

"The way to stop violence in America is to stop spanking children," argues psychologist John Valusek. In a speech to the Utah Association for Mental Health some weeks ago, Valusek declared that parental spanking promotes the thesis that violence against others is acceptable.
"Spanking is the first half-inch on the yardstick of violence," said Valusek. "It is followed by hitting and ultimately by rape, murder, and assassination. The modeling behavior that occurs at home sets the stage: 'I will resort to violence when I don't know what else to do.' "[3]

How ridiculous it seems to blame America's obsession with violence on the disciplinary efforts of loving parents! This conclusion is especially foolish in view of the bloody fare offered to our children on television each day. The average sixteen-year-old has watched 18,000 murders during his formative years, including a daily bombardment of knifings, shootings, hangings, decapitations, and general dismemberment. Thus, it does seem strange that the psychological wizards of our day search elsewhere for the cause of brutality—and eventually point the finger of blame at the parents who are diligently training our future responsible citizens. Yet this is the kind of "press" that has been given in recent years to parents who believe in spanking their disobedient children.

Opposition to corporal punishment can be summarized by four common arguments, all of them based on error and misunderstanding. The first is represented by Dr. Valusek's statement, and assumes that spankings teach children to hit and hurt others. It depicts corporal punishment as a hostile physical attack by an angry parent whose purpose is to damage or inflict harm on his little victim. Admittedly, that kind of violence does occur regularly between generations and is tremendously destructive to children. However, corporal punishment in the hands of a loving parent is altogether different in purpose and practice. It is a teaching tool by which harmful behavior is inhibited, rather than a wrathful attempt by one person to damage another. One is an act of love; the other is an act of hostility, and they are as different as night and day.

I responded to Dr. Valusek's argument in my previous book, *Hide or Seek*, showing the place of minor pain in teaching children to behave responsibly:

> Those same specialists also say that a spanking teaches your child to hit others, making him a more violent person. Nonsense! If your child has ever bumped his arm against a hot stove, you can bet he'll never deliberately do that again. He does not become a more violent person because the stove burnt him. In fact, he learned a valuable lesson from the pain. Similarly, when he falls out of his high chair or smashes his finger in the door or is bitten by a grumpy dog, he learns about the physical dangers in his world. These bumps and bruises throughout childhood are nature's way of teaching him that the physical world around him must be respected. They do not damage his self-esteem. They do not make him vicious. They merely acquaint him with reality. In like manner, an appropriate spanking from a loving parent in a moment of defiance provides the same service. It tells him there are not only physical dangers to be avoided, but he must steer clear of some social traps as well (selfishness, defiance, dishonesty, unprovoked aggression. etc.).[4]

The second rationale against corporal punishment can also be found in Dr. Valusek's concluding sentence, "I will resort to violence (spankings) when I don't know what else to do." Do you see the subtlety of this quotation? It characterizes a spanking as an absolute last resort—as the final act of exasperation and frustration. As such, it comes on the heels of screaming, threatening, hand-wringing, and buckets of tears. Even those authorities who recommend corporal punishment often fall into this trap, suggesting that it be applied only when all else has failed. I couldn't disagree more strongly.

A spanking is to be reserved for use in response to willful defiance, *whenever it occurs.* Period! It is much more effective to apply it early in the conflict, while the parent's emotional apparatus is still under control, than after ninety minutes of scratching and clawing. In fact, child abuse is more likely to occur when a little youngster is permitted to irritate and agitate and sass and disobey and pout for hours, until finally the parent's anger reaches a point of explosion where anything can happen (and often does). Professionals like Dr. Valusek have inadvertently contributed to violence against children, in my view, because they have stripped parents of the right to correct children's routine behavior problems while they are of minor irritation. Then when these small frustrations accumulate, the parent does (as Valusek said) "resort to violence when he doesn't know what else to do."

The third common argument against spanking comes from the findings of animal psychology. If a mouse is running in a maze, he will learn much faster if the experimenter rewards his correct turns with food than he will if his incorrect choices are punished with a mild electric shock. From this and similar studies has come the incredible assumption that punishment has little influence on human behavior. But human beings are not mice, and it is naive to equate them simplistically. Obviously, a child is capable of rebellious and defiant attitudes which have no relevance to a puzzled mouse sitting at a crossroads in a maze. I agree that it would not help boys and girls learn to read by shocking them for each mispronounced word. On the other hand, deliberate disobedience involves the child's perception of parental authority and his obligations to accept it (whereas the mouse does not even know the experimenter exists).

If punishment doesn't influence human behavior, then why is the issuance of speeding citations by police so effective in controlling traffic on a busy street? Why, then, do homeowners rush to get their tax payments in the mail to avoid a 6 percent penalty for being late? If punishment has no power, then why does a well-deserved spanking often turn a sullen little troublemaker into a sweet and loving angel? Rat psychology notwithstanding, both reward and punishment play an important role in shaping human behavior, and neither should be discounted. Leonardo da Vinci hadn't heard about the mouse in the maze when he wrote, "He who does not punish evil commands it to be done!"

The fourth argument against the judicious practice of spanking comes from those who see it as damaging to the dignity and self-worth of the child. Suffice it to say at this point that a child is fully capable of discerning whether his parent is conveying love or hatred. This is why the youngster who knows he deserves a spanking appears almost relieved when it finally comes. Rather than being insulted by the discipline, he understands its purpose and appreciates the control it gives him over his own impulses.

This childish comprehension was beautifully illustrated by a father who told me of a time when his five-year-old son was disobeying in a restaurant. This lad was sassing his mother, flipping water on his younger brother, and deliberately making a nuisance of himself. After four warnings went unheeded, the father took his son by the arm and marched him to the parking lot where he proceeded to administer a spanking. Watching this episode was a meddling woman who had followed them out of the restaurant and into the parking lot. When the punishment began, she shook her finger at the father and screamed, "Leave that boy alone! Turn him loose! If you don't stop I'm going to call the police!" The five-year-old, who had been crying and jumping, immediately stopped yelling and said to his father in surprise, "What's wrong with that woman, Dad?" He understood the purpose for the discipline, even if the "rescuer" didn't. I only wish that Dr. Valusek and his contemporaries were as perceptive as this child.

Let me hasten to emphasize that corporal punishment is not the only tool for use in shaping the will, nor is it appropriate at all ages and for all situations. The wise parent must understand the physical and emotional characteristics of each stage in childhood, and then fit the discipline to a boy's or girl's individual needs.[5]

Can you provide some "ground-rules" for the use of corporal punishment for strong-willed toddlers?
Mild spankings can begin between fifteen and eighteen months

of age. They should be relatively infrequent, and must be reserved for clear defiance, not childish irresponsibility. A heavy hand of authority during this period causes the child to suppress his need to experiment and test his environment, which can have long lasting consequences. The toddler should be taught to obey and yield to parental leadership, but that end result will not be accomplished overnight.

When spankings occur, they should be administered with a neutral object; that is, with a small switch or belt, but rarely with the hand. I have always felt that the hand should be seen by the child as an object of love rather than an instrument of punishment. Furthermore, if a parent commonly slaps a youngster when he is not expecting to be hit, then he will probably duck and flinch whenever Father suddenly scratches his ear. And, of course, a slap in the face can reposition the nose or do permanent damage to the ears or jaw. If all spankings are administered with a neutral object, applied where intended, then the child need never fear that he will suddenly be chastised for some accidental indiscretion. (There are exceptions to this rule, such as when a child's hands are slapped or thumped for reaching for a stove or other dangerous object.)

Should a spanking hurt? Yes, or else it will have no influence. A swat on the behind through three layers of wet diapers simply conveys no urgent message. However, a small amount of pain for a young child goes a long way; it is certainly not necessary to lash or "whip" him. Two or three stinging strokes on the legs or bottom with a switch are usually sufficient to emphasize the point, "You must obey me." And finally, it is important to spank *immediately* after the offense, or not at all. A toddler's memory is not sufficiently developed to permit even a ten-minute delay in the administration of justice. Then after the episode is over and the tears have subsided, the child might want to be held and reassured by his mother or father. By all means, let him come. Embrace him in the security of your loving arms. Rock him softly. Tell him how much you love him and why he must "mind his mommie." This moment can be the most important event in the entire day. And for the Christian family, it is extremely important to pray with the child at that time, admitting to God we have *all* sinned and no one is perfect. Divine forgiveness is a marvelous experience, even for a very young child.[6]

How long do you think a child should be allowed to cry after being punished or spanked? Is there a limit?
Yes, I believe there should be a limit. As long as the tears represent a genuine release of emotion, they should be permitted to fall. But crying quickly changes from inner sobbing to an exterior weapon. It becomes a tool of protest to punish the enemy. Real crying usually lasts two minutes or less, but may continue for five. After that point, the child is merely complaining, and the change can be recognized in the tone and intensity of his voice. I would require him to stop the protest crying, usually by offering him a little more of whatever caused the original tears. For the younger child, the crying can easily be stopped by getting him interested in something else.[7]

I have spanked my children for their disobedience and it didn't seem to help. Does this approach fail with some children?
Children are so tremendously variable that it is sometimes hard to believe that they are all members of the same human family. Some children can be crushed with nothing more than a stern look; others seem to require strong and even painful disciplinary measures to make a vivid impression. This difference usually results from the degree to which a child needs adult approval and acceptance. The primary parental task is to get behind the eyes of the child, thereby tailoring the discipline to his unique perception.

In a direct answer to your question, it is not this individual variation that causes spanking to be ineffectual in most cases. When disciplinary measures fail, it is usually because of fundamental errors in their application. It is possible for twice the amount of punishment to yield half the results. I have made a study of situations where the parent has told me that the child ignores the spankings he receives, going back to violate the same rule. There are four basic reasons for the lack of success:

1. The most recurring problem results from infrequent, whimsical punishment. Half the time the child is not punished for a particular act of defiance; the other half of the time he is held accountable for it. Children need to know the certainty of justice.

2. The child may be more strong-willed than the parent, and they both know it. If he can outlast a temporary onslaught, he has won a major battle, eliminating punishment as a tool in the

parent's repertoire. Even though Mom spanks him, he wins the battle by defying her again. The solution to this situation is obvious: outlast him; win, even if it takes a repeated measure. The experience will be painful for both participants, but the benefits will come tomorrow and tomorrow and tomorrow.

3. The parent suddenly decides to employ this form of punishment after doing nothing for a year or two prior to that time. It takes a child a while to respond to a new procedure in this manner, and the parent might get discouraged during the adjustment period.

4. The spanking may be too gentle. If it doesn't hurt, it isn't worth avoiding next time. A slap with the hand on the bottom of a multi-diapered thirty-month-old is not a deterrent to anything. It isn't necessary to beat a child, certainly, but he should be able to "feel" the message.

There *are* some children for whom spankings do not work. Notably, I've seen hyperactive children who are greatly agitated by any response which excites their nervous system. In these and related cases, other forms of discipline must be applied.[8]

Is my ten-year-old too old to be spanked?

Physical punishment should be relatively infrequent during the period immediately prior to adolescence. Of course, some strong-willed children absolutely demand to be spanked, and their wishes should be granted. However, the compliant youngster should have experienced his last woodshed experience by the end of his first decade (or even four years earlier).[9]

I would like to hear your views about disciplining a teenager, especially since you say spanking him is neither wise nor productive.

Your only tool of discipline is to manipulate your teenager's environmental circumstances in moments of confrontation. You have the keys to the family automobile and can allow your son or daughter to use it (or be chauffeured in it). You may grant or withhold privileges, including permission to go to a party. You control the family purse and can choose to share it or loan it or dole it or close it. And you can "ground" your adolescent or deny him the use of the telephone or television for awhile.

Now obviously, these are not very influential "motivators,"

and are at times totally inadequate for the situation at hand. After we have appealed to reason and cooperation and family loyalty, all that remains are relatively weak methods of "punishment." We can only link behavior of our kids with desirable and undesirable consequences and hope the connection will be of sufficient influence to elicit their cooperation.

If that sounds pretty wobbly-legged, let me admit what I am implying: a willful, angry sixteen-year-old boy or girl *can* win a confrontation with his or her parents today, if worst comes to worst. The law leans ever more in the direction of emancipation of the teenager. He can leave home in many areas and avoid being returned. He can drink and smoke pot and break many other civil laws before he is punished by society. His girl friend can obtain birth control pills in many states without her parents' knowledge or permission. And if that fails, she can slip into a clinic for an unannounced abortion. Very few "adult" privileges and vices can be denied a teenager who has the passion for independence and a will to fight.

How different was the situation when Billy-Joe was raised on the farm in days of old, living perhaps eight or ten miles by horseback from the home of his nearest contemporary. His dad, Farmer Brown, impressed by his own authority, could "talk sense" to his rebellious boy without the interference of outside pressures. There is no doubt that it was much easier for father and son to come to terms while sitting on a plow at the far end of Forgotten Field.

But today, every spark of adolescent discontent is fanned into a smoldering flame. The grab for the teen dollar has become big business, with enticing magazines, record companies, radio, television, and concert entrepreneurs to cater to each youthful whim. And, of course, masses of high school students congregate idly in the city and patronize those obliging companies. They have become a force to be considered.

Unless teenagers have an inner tug toward cooperation and responsibility, the situation can get nasty very quickly. But where does that voice of restraint originate? It has been my contention that the early years of childhood are vital to the establishment of respect between generations. Without that kind of foundation—without a touch of awe in the child's perception of his parent—then the balance of power and control is definitely shifted toward the younger combatant. I would be doing a disservice to my readers if I implied otherwise.[10]

SIBLING
RIVALRY

**Nothing irritates me as much as the fighting and
bickering that occurs between my two boys. Do all
parents struggle with sibling conflict or does it result
from failure on my part?**

If American women were asked to indicate *the* most irritating
feature of child rearing, I'm convinced that sibling rivalry would
get their unanimous vote. Little children (and older ones, too)
are not content just to hate each other in private. They attack
one another like miniature warriors, mobilizing their troops and
probing for a weakness in the defensive line. They argue, hit,
kick, scream, grab toys, taunt, tattle, and sabotage the opposing
forces. I knew one child who deeply resented being sick with a
cold while his older sibling was healthy, so he secretly blew his
nose on the mouthpiece of his brother's musical instrument!
The big loser from such combat, of course, is the harassed
mother who must listen to the noise of the battlefield and then
try to patch up the wounded. If her emotional nature requires
peace and tranquility (and most women do), she may stagger
under the barrage of cannonfire.

Columnist Ann Landers recently asked her readers to respond
to the question, "If you had known then what you know now,
would you have had children?" Among ten thousand women
who answered, 70 percent said No! A subsequent survey by
Good Housekeeping posed the same question and 95 percent of
the respondents answered Yes. It is impossible to explain the
contradictory results from these two inquiries, although the
accompanying comments were enlightening. One unidentified
woman wrote, "Would I have children again? A thousand times,
No! My children have completely destroyed my life, my

marriage, and my identity as a person. There are no joys.
Prayers don't help—nothing stops a 'screaming kid.' "

It is my contention that something *will* stop a screaming kid,
or even a dozen of them. It is not necessary or healthy to allow
children to destroy each other and make life miserable for the
adults around them. Sibling rivalry is difficult to "cure" but it
can certainly be treated.[1]

What causes sibling rivalry?

Sibling rivalry is not new, of course. It was responsible for the
first murder on record (when Cain killed Abel), and has been
represented in virtually every two-child family from that time to
this. The underlying source of this conflict is old-fashioned
jealousy and competition between children. Marguerite and
Willard Beecher, writing in their book *Parents on the Run*,[2]
expressed the inevitability of this struggle as follows:

> It was once believed that if parents would explain to a child
> that he was having a little brother or sister, he would not
> resent it. He was told that his parents had enjoyed him so
> much that they wanted to increase their happiness. This
> was supposed to avoid jealous competition and rivalry. It
> did not work. Why should it? Needless to say, if a man tells
> his wife he has loved her so much that he now plans to
> bring another wife into the home to "increase his
> happiness," she would not be immune to jealousy. On the
> contrary, the fight would just begin—in exactly the same
> fashion as it does with children.[3]

If jealousy between kids is so common, then how can parents minimize the natural antagonism which children feel for their siblings?

The first step is to avoid circumstances which compare them
unfavorably with each other. Lecturer Bill Gothard has stated
that the root of all feelings of inferiority is comparison. I agree.
The question is not "How am I doing?" it is "How am I doing
compared with John or Steven or Marion?" The issue is not how
fast can I run, but who crosses the finish line first. A boy does
not care how tall he is; he is vitally interested in "who is tallest."

Each child systematically measures himself against his peers,
and is tremendously sensitive to failure within his own family.

Accordingly, parents should guard against comparative statements which routinely favor one child over another. This is particularly true in three areas.

First, children are extremely sensitive about the matter of physical attractiveness and body characteristics. It is highly inflammatory to commend one child at the expense of the other. Suppose, for example, that Sharon is permitted to hear the casual remark about her sister, "Betty is sure going to be a gorgeous girl." The very fact that Sharon was not mentioned will probably establish the two girls as rivals. If there is a significant difference in beauty between the two, you can be assured that Sharon has already concluded, "Yeah, I'm the ugly one." When her fears are then confirmed by her parents, resentment and jealousy are generated.

Beauty is *the* most significant factor in the self-esteem of Western children, as I attempted to express in *Hide or Seek*. Anything that a parent utters on this subject within the hearing of children should be screened carefully. It has the power to make brothers and sisters hate one another.

Second, the matter of intelligence is another sensitive nerve to be handled with care. It is not uncommon to hear parents say in front of their children, "I think the younger boy is actually brighter than his brother." Adults find it difficult to comprehend how powerful that kind of assessment can be in a child's mind. Even when the comments are unplanned and are spoken routinely, they convey how a child is "seen" within his family. We are all vulnerable to that bit of evidence.

Third, children (and especially boys) are extremely competitive with regard to athletic abilities. Those who are slower, weaker, and less coordinated than their brothers are rarely able to accept "second best" with grace and dignity. Consider, for example, the following note given to me by the mother of two boys. It was written by her nine-year-old son to his eight-year-old brother, the evening after the younger child had beaten him in a race.

Dear Jim:

I am the greatest and your the badest. And I can beat everybody in a race and you can't beat anybody in a race. I'm the smartest and your the dumbest. I'm the best sport player and your the badest sport player. And your also a hog. I can beat anybody up. And that's the truth. And that's the end of this story.

Yours truly,
Richard

This note is humorous to me, because Richard's motive was so poorly disguised. He had been badly stung by his humiliation on the field of honor, so he came home and raised the battle flags. He will probably spend the next eight weeks looking for opportunities to fire torpedoes into Jim's soft underbelly. Such is the nature of mankind.[4]

Are you suggesting that parents eliminate all aspects of individuality within family life or that healthy competition should be discouraged in order to minimize the jealousy factor between children?
Definitely not. I am saying that in matters relative to beauty, brains, and athletic ability, each child should know that in his parents' eyes, he is respected and has equal worth with his siblings.

Praise and criticism *at home* should be distributed as evenly as possible, although some children will inevitably be more successful in the outside world. And finally, we should remember that children do not build fortresses around strengths—they construct them to protect weakness. Thus, when a child like Richard begins to brag and boast and attack his siblings, he is revealing the threats he feels at that point. Our sensitivity to those signals will help minimize the potential for jealousy within our children.[5]

Sometimes I feel as though my children fight and argue as a method of attracting my attention. If this is the case, how should I respond?
You are probably correct in making that assumption. Sibling rivalry often represents a form of manipulation of parents. Quarreling and fighting provide an opportunity for both children to "capture" adult attention. It has been written, "Some children had rather be wanted for murder than not wanted at all." Toward this end, a pair of obnoxious kids can tacitly agree to bug their parents until they get a response— even if it is an angry reaction.

One father told me recently that his son and his nephew began to argue and then beat each other with their fists. Both fathers were nearby and decided to let the fight run its natural course. During the first lull in the action one of the boys glanced sideways toward the passive men and said, "Isn't anybody going to stop us before we get hurt?!" The fight, you see, was something neither boy wanted. Their violent combat was directly related to the presence of the two adults and would have taken a different form if the boys had been alone. Children will often "hook" their parents' attention and intervention in this way.

Believe it or not, this form of sibling rivalry is easiest to control. The parent must simply render the behavior unprofitable to each participant. I would recommend that you review the problem (for example, a morning full of bickering) with the children, and then say, "Now listen carefully. If the two of you want to pick on each other and make yourselves miserable, then be my guest [assuming there is a fairly equal balance of power between them]. Go outside and fight until you're exhausted. But it's not going to occur under my feet anymore. It's over! And you know that I mean business when I make that kind of statement. Do we understand each other?"

Having made the boundaries clear, I would act decisively the *instant* either boy returned to his bickering. If I had separate bedrooms, I would confine one child to each room for at least thirty minutes of complete boredom—without radio or television. Or I would assign one to clean the garage and the other to mow the lawn. Or I would make them take a nap. My avowed purpose would be to make them believe me the next time I submitted a request for peace and tranquility.

What is most surprising is that children are happiest when their parents enforce these reasonable limits with love and dignity. Instead of wringing their hands and crying and begging and screaming (which actually reinforces the disruptive behavior and makes it worse), a mother or father should approach the conflict with dignity and self-control.[6]

I've been very careful to be fair with my children and give them no reason to resent one another. Nevertheless, they continue to fight. What can I do?

The problem may rest in your lack of disciplinary control at home. Sibling rivalry is at its worst when there is an inadequate system of justice among children—where the "lawbreakers" do not get caught, or if apprehended are set free without standing trial. It is important to understand that laws in a society are established and enforced for the purpose of protecting people from each other. Likewise, a family is a mini-society with the same requirement for protection of human rights.

For purposes of illustration, suppose that I live in a community where there is no established law. Policemen do not exist and there are no courts to whom disagreements can be appealed. Under those circumstances, my neighbor and I can abuse each other with impunity. He can take my lawnmower and throw rocks through my windows, while I steal the peaches from his favorite tree and dump my leaves over his fence. This kind of mutual antagonism has a way of escalating day by day, becoming ever more violent with the passage of time. When permitted to run its natural course, as in early American history, the end result can be feudal hatred and murder.

As indicated, individual families are similar to societies in their need for law and order. In the absence of justice, "neighboring" siblings begin to assault one another. The older child is bigger and tougher, which allows him to oppress his younger brothers and sister. But the junior member of the family is not without weapons of his own. He strikes back by breaking the toys and prized possessions of the older sibling and interferes when friends are visiting. Mutual hatred then erupts like an angry volcano, spewing its destructive contents on everyone in its path.

Nevertheless, when the children appeal to their parents for intervention, they are often left to fight it out among themselves. In many homes, the parents do not have sufficient disciplinary control to enforce their judgments. In others, they are so exasperated with constant bickering among siblings that they refuse to get involved. In still others, parents require an older child to live with an admitted injustice "because your brother is smaller than you." Thus, they tie his hands and render him utterly defenseless against the mischief of his bratty little brother or sister. Even more commonly today, mothers and fathers are both working while their children are home busily disassembling each other.

I will say it again to parents: one of your most important responsibilities is to establish an equitable system of justice and a balance of power at home. There should be reasonable "laws" which are enforced fairly for each member of the family. For purposes of illustration, let me list the boundaries and rules which have evolved through the years in my own home.

1. Neither child is ever allowed to make fun of the other in a destructive way. Period! This is an inflexible rule with no exceptions.

2. Each child's room is his private territory. There are locks on both doors, and permission to enter is a revokable privilege. (Families with more than one child in each bedroom can allocate available living space for each youngster.)

3. The older child is not permitted to tease the younger child.

4. The younger child is forbidden to harass the older child.

5. The children are not required to play with each other when they prefer to be alone or with other friends.

6. We mediate any genuine conflict as quickly as possible, being careful to show impartiality and extreme fairness.

As with any plan of justice, this plan requires (1) children's respect for leadership of the parent, (2) willingness by the parent to mediate, (3) occasional enforcement or punishment. When this approach is accomplished with love, the emotional tone of the home can be changed from one of hatred to (at least) tolerance.[7]

My older child is a great student and earns straight A's year after year. Her younger sister, now in the sixth grade, is completely bored in school and won't even try. The frustrating thing is that the younger girl is probably brighter than her older sister. Why would she refuse to apply her ability like this?

There could be many reasons for her academic disinterest, but let me suggest the most probable explanation. Children will often refuse to compete when they think they are likely to place second instead of first. Therefore, a younger child may diligently avoid challenging an older sibling in his area of greatest strength. If Son Number One is a great athlete, then Son Number Two may be more interested in collecting butterflies. If Daughter Number One is a disciplined pianist, then Daughter Number Two may be a boy-crazy goof-off.

This rule does not always hold, of course, depending on the child's fear of failure and the way he estimates his chances of successful competition. If his confidence is high, he may blatantly wade into the territory owned by big brother, determined to do even better. However, the more typical response is to seek new areas of compensation which are not yet dominated by a family superstar.

If this explanation fits the behavior of your younger daughter, then it would be wise to accept something less than perfection from her school performance. Every child need not fit the same mold—nor can we force them to do so.[8]

(The following excerpt was taken from an actual letter sent to me by a creative mother.)

You recommended in *Dare to Discipline* and *Hide or Seek* that we use a monetary reward system to encourage our children to accept new responsibilities. This approach has helped a great deal and our family is functioning much smoother. However, I had an idea for improving the system which has worked beautifully with my two boys, ages six and eight. In order for them to earn a reward for brushing their teeth, making their beds, putting away their clothes, etc., they both must complete the jobs as assigned. In other words, I tax them both for one child's failure and reward them both for mutual successes. They got in the spirit of working together to achieve the goal. It has made them business partners, in a sense. I thought you would be interested in this approach. This mother has done what I hope other parents will do: use my writings as a springboard to creative approaches of their own. My illustrations merely show that the most successful parents are those who find unique solutions to the routine problems of living. The writer of this letter has done that beautifully.[9]

We are planning our family very carefully, and want to space the children properly. Is there an ideal age span that will bring greater harmony between them?
Children who are two years apart and of the same sex are more likely to be competitive with one another. On the other hand, they are also more likely to enjoy mutual companionship. If you produce your babies four or more years apart there will be less camaraderie between them but at least you'll have only one child in college at a time. My evasive reply to your question reflects my personal bias: There are many more important reasons for planning a baby at a particular time than the age of

those already born. Of greater significance is the health of the mother, the desire for another child, financial considerations, and the stability of the marriage. The relative ages of siblings is not one of the major determiners, in my opinion.[10]

Before our new baby was born last month, our three-year-old son was thrilled at the prospect of a baby brother or sister. Now, however, he shows signs of jealousy, sucking his thumb sullenly when I nurse the baby, and getting very loud and silly when friends drop in to bring a gift to the new arrival. Please suggest some ways I can ease him through this period of adjustment.

Your son is revealing a "textbook" reaction to the invasion that has occurred in his private kingdom. We saw a similar response when our second child was born. Our son arrived on the scene when his sister was five years of age. She had been the only granddaughter on either side of the family and had received all the adult attention that can be heaped upon a child. Then suddenly, her secure palace was invaded by a cute little fellow who captured and held center stage. All of the relatives cuddled, cooed, rocked, bounced, and hugged baby Ryan, while Danae watched suspiciously from the wings. As we drove home from Grandmother's house on a Sunday afternoon, about a week after Ryan's arrival, our daughter suddenly said, "Daddy, you know I'm just talking. You know, I don't mean to be bad or anything, but sometimes I wish little Ryan wasn't here!"

She had given us a valuable clue to her feelings in that brief sentence, and we immediately seized the opportunity she had provided. We moved her into the front seat of the car so we could discuss what she had said. We told her we understood how she felt and assured her of our love. We also explained that a baby is completely helpless and will die if people don't take care of him—feed, clothe, change, and love him. We reminded her that she was taken care of that way when she was a baby, and explained that Ryan would soon grow up, too. We were also careful in the months that followed to minimize the threat to her place in our hearts. By giving careful attention to her feelings and security, the relationship with her brother developed into a lasting friendship and love.

Danae's admission was not a typical response among children. Much more commonly, a child will be unable or unwilling to express the insecurity brought by a newborn rival.

requiring his parents to read more subtle signs and cues. The most reliable symptoms of the I've-been-replaced syndrome is a sudden return to infantile behavior. Obviously, "If babyhood is where it's at, then I'll be a baby again." Therefore, the child throws temper tantrums, wets the bed, sucks his thumb, holds tightly to Momma, baby talks, etc. In this situation, the child has observed a clear and present danger and is solving it in the best way he knows.

If your firstborn child seems to feel like a has-been, I would suggest the following procedures be implemented:

1. Bring his feelings out in the open and help him verbalize them. When a child is acting silly in front of adults, trying to make them laugh or notice him, it is good to take him in your arms and say, "What's the matter, Joey? Do you need some attention today?" Gradually, a child can be taught to use similar words when he feels excluded or rejected. "I need some attention, Dad. Will you play with me?" By verbalizing his feelings, you also help him understand himself better.

2. Don't let antisocial behavior succeed. If the child cries when the baby-sitter arrives, leave him anyway. A temper tantrum can be greeted with a firm swat, etc. However, reveal little anger and displeasure, remembering that the entire episode is motivated by a threat to your love.

3. Meet his needs in ways that grant status to him for being older. Take him to the park, making it clear that the baby is too little to go; talk "up" to him about the things he can do that the baby can't—he can use the bathroom instead of his pants, for example. Let him help take care of the baby so he will feel he is part of the family process.

Beyond these corrective steps, give your son some time to adjust to his new situation. Even though it stresses him somewhat today, he should profit from the realization that he does not sit at the center of the universe.[11]

TEACHING CHILDREN TO BE RESPONSIBLE

You have indicated that a child's willful defiance should be handled differently than mere childish irresponsibility. I'm not sure I understand the distinction between these two categories of behavior. Can you explain them further?

Willful defiance, as the name implies, is a deliberate act of disobedience. It occurs only when the child knows what his parents expect and then is determined to do the opposite. In short, it is a refusal to accept parental leadership, such as running away when called, screaming insults, acts of outright disobedience, etc. By contrast, childish irresponsibility results from forgetting, accidents, mistakes, a short attention span, a low frustration tolerance, and immaturity. In the first instance, the child knows he was wrong and is waiting to see what his parent can do about it; in the second, he has simply blundered into a consequence he did not plan. It is wrong, in my view, to resort to corporal punishment for the purpose of instilling responsibility (unless, of course, the child has defiantly refused to accept it).

Ultimately, the appropriate disciplinary reaction by a mother or father should be determined entirely by the matter of *intention*. Suppose my three-year-old son is standing in the doorway and I say, "Ryan, please shut the door." But in his linguistic immaturity he misunderstands my request and opens the door even further. Will I punish him for disobeying me? Of course not, even though he did the opposite of what I asked. He may never even know that he failed the assignment. My tolerance is dictated by his intention. He honestly tried to obey me.

However, if when I ask Ryan to pick up his toys, he stamps his little foot and screams, "No!" before throwing a Tonka truck in my direction—then I am obligated to accept his challenge. In short, my child is never so likely to be punished as when I'm sure *he knows* he deserves it.

The Bible teaches quite clearly that human beings have a universal tendency toward rebellion and that must be dealt with during childhood when it is focused primarily upon the parents. If that defiance is not suppressed in the tender years, it may develop into general rebellion against all authority, including that of God Himself. Our Creator has warned of the consequences of this rebellion, stating in Proverbs 29:1, "He, that being often reproved hardeneth his neck, shall suddenly be destroyed, and that without remedy" (KJV). Thus, we should teach our children to submit to our loving leadership as preparation for their later life of obedience to God.[1]

How should parents deal with childish irresponsibility when it involves neither defiance nor passive aggression?
Kids love games of all sorts, especially if adults will get involved with them. It is often possible to turn a teaching situation into a fun activity which "sensitizes" the entire family to the issue you're trying to teach. Let me tell you how we taught our children to put their napkins in their laps before eating. We tried reminding them for two or three years, but simply weren't getting through. Then we turned it into a family game.

Now, if one of the Dobsons takes a single bite of food before putting his napkin in his lap, he is required to go to his bedroom and count to twenty-five in a loud voice. This game is highly effective, although it has some definite disadvantages. You can't imagine how foolish Shirley and I feel when we're standing in an empty section of the house, counting to twenty-five while our children giggle. Ryan, particularly, *never* forgets his napkin and he loves to catch the rest of us in a moment of preoccupation. He will sit perfectly still, looking straight ahead until the first bite of food goes in. Then he wheels toward the offender, points his finger, and says, "Gotcha!"

For all of those many parenting objectives that involve teaching responsibility (rather than conquering willful defiance), game-playing should be considered as the method of choice.[2]

Do you think a child should be required to say "thank you" and "please" around the house?

I sure do. Requiring these phrases is one method of reminding the child that this is not a "gimmie-gimmie" world. Even though his mother is cooking for him and buying for him and giving to him, he must assume a few attitudinal responsibilities in return. Appreciation must be taught and this instructional process begins with fundamental politeness at home.[3]

My ten-year-old can be the most irresponsible kid I've ever known. He hates to work and he has lost or broken everything of value he's ever been given. I've read many books about teaching children to be mature and responsible, and we're working on these objectives. My problem is that I lose my patience with him too often. I yell at him and accuse him of being stupid and lazy. Then I feel terrible about my lack of control. Am I damaging his self-esteem by these outbursts?

Children are usually very resilient and most of them can absorb occasional parental outbursts without sustaining permanent harm. In fact, your displeasure is part of the teaching process whereby a parent nudges his child in the direction of maturity. However, if you realize you are over-reacting frequently or habitually, especially if it involves labeling him unfairly, you would do well to remember what someone has said about the way people perceive themselves:

We are not what we think we are . . .

We are not even what *others* think we are . . .

We are what we *think* others think we are.

There is great truth in this statement. Each of us evaluates what we believe our associates are thinking about us, and then we often play that prescribed role. This explains why we wear a very different "face" with different groups. A doctor may be an unsmiling professional with his patients, being reserved and wise in their presence. They "see" him that way and he complies. That evening, however, he is reunited with his former college friends who remember him as a postadolescent screwball. His personality may oscillate 180 degrees between afternoon and night, being totally unrecognizable if seen by an amazed patient. Similarly, most of us *are* what we think others think we are.

That being true, your child will conform to the image he

thinks you hold of him. If you call him lazy and stupid, his behavior will prove that assessment to be correct. Fortunately, the opposite is also true. So whenever possible, control your impulsive reactions and give him a high image to shoot for. Otherwise, he will stoop to match the one you are now communicating.

I know! I know! It sounds easy on paper, but it is tough to implement. I have trouble following this advice, too. But we can at least *try* to provide what our imperfect kids need from us imperfect parents.

Must I brag on my child all day for every little thing he does? Isn't it possible to create a spoiled brat by telling him his every move is wonderful?

Yes, inflationary praise is unnecessary. Junior quickly catches on to your verbal game, and your words then lose their meaning. It is helpful to distinguish between the concepts of *flattery* versus *praise*. Flattery is unearned. It is what Grandma says when she comes for a visit: "Oh, look at my beautiful little girl! You're getting prettier each day. I'll bet you'll have to beat the boys off with a club when you get to be a teenager!" Or, "My, what a smart boy you are." Flattery occurs when you heap compliments upon the child for something he did not achieve.

Praise, on the other hand, is used to reinforce positive, constructive behavior. It should be highly specific rather than general. "You've been a good boy . . ." is unsatisfactory. "I like the way you kept your room straight today," is better. Parents should always watch for opportunities to offer genuine, well-deserved praise to their children, while avoiding empty flattery.

How can I acquaint my junior higher with the need for responsible behavior throughout his life? He is desperately in need of this understanding.

The overall objective during the preadolescent period is to teach the child that his actions have inevitable consequences. One of the most serious casualties in a permissive society is the failure to connect those two factors, behavior and consequences. Too often, a three-year-old child screams insults at his mother, but Mom stands blinking her eyes in confusion. A first grader launches an attack on his teacher, but the school makes allowances for his age and takes no action. A ten-year-old is caught stealing candy in a store, but is released to the recognizance of his parents. A fifteen-year-old sneaks the keys to the family car, but his father pays the fine when is he arrested. A seventeen-year-old drives his Chevy like a maniac and his parents pay for the repairs when he wraps it around a telephone pole. You see, all through childhood, loving parents seem determined to intervene between behavior and consequences, breaking the connection and preventing the valuable learning that could have occurred.

Thus, it is possible for a young man or woman to enter adult life, not really knowing that life bites—that every move we make directly affects our future—that irresponsible behavior eventually produces sorrow and pain. Such a person applies for his first job and arrives late for work three times during the first week; then, when he is fired in a flurry of hot words, he becomes bitter and frustrated. It was the first time in his life that Mom and Dad couldn't come running to rescue him from the unpleasant consequences. (Unfortunately, many American parents still try to "bail out" the grown children even when they are in their twenties and live away from home.) What is the result? This overprotection produces emotional cripples who often develop lasting characteristics of dependency and a kind of perpetual adolescence.

How does one connect behavior with consequences? By being willing to let the child experience a reasonable amount of pain or inconvenience when he behaves irresponsibly. When Jack misses the school bus through his own dawdling, let him walk a mile or two and enter school in midmorning (unless safety factors prevent this). If Janie carelessly loses her lunch money, let her skip a meal. Obviously, it is possible to carry this principle too far, being harsh and inflexible with an immature child. But the best approach is to expect boys and girls to carry the responsibility that is appropriate for their age, and occasionally to taste the bitter fruit that irresponsibility bears.[5]

I have a horrible time getting my ten-year-old daughter ready to catch the school bus each morning. She will get up when I insist, but she dawdles and plays as soon as I leave the room. I have to goad and push and warn her every few minutes or else she will be late. So I get more and more angry, and usually end up by screaming insults at her. I know this is not the best way to handle the little

brat, but I declare, she makes me want to clobber her. Tell me how I can get her moving without this emotion every day.

You are playing right into your daughter's hands by assuming the responsibility for getting her ready each morning. A ten-year-old should definitely be able to handle that task on her own steam, but your anger is not likely to bring it about. We had a very similar problem with our own daughter when she was ten. Perhaps the solution we worked out will be helpful to you.

Danae's morning time problem related primarily to her compulsivity about her room. She will not leave for school each day unless her bed is made perfectly and every trinket is in its proper place. This was not something we taught her; she has always been very meticulous about her possessions. (I should add that her brother, Ryan, does not have that problem.) Danae could easily finish these tasks on time if she were motivated to do so, but she was never in a particular hurry. Therefore, my wife began to fall into the same habit you described, warning, threatening, pushing, shoving, and ultimately becoming angry as the clock moved toward the deadline.

Shirley and I discussed the problem and agreed that there had to be a better method of getting through the morning. I subsequently created a system which we called "Checkpoints." It worked like this. Danae was instructed to be out of bed and standing erect before 6:30 each morning. It was her responsibility to set her own clock-radio and get herself out of bed. If she succeeded in getting up on time (even one minute later was considered a missed item) she immediately went to the kitchen where a chart was taped to the refrigerator door. She then circled "yes" or "no," with regard to the first checkpoint for that date. It couldn't be more simple. She either did or did not get up by 6:30.

The second checkpoint occurred forty minutes later at 7:10. By that time, she was required to have her room straightened to her own satisfaction, be dressed and have her teeth brushed, hair combed, etc., and be ready to begin practicing the piano. Forty minutes was ample time for these tasks, which could actually be done in ten or fifteen minutes if she wanted to hurry. Thus, the only way she could miss the second checkpoint was to ignore it deliberately.

Now, what meaning did the checkpoints have? Did failure to meet them bring anger and wrath and gnashing of teeth? Of course not. The consequences were straightforward and fair. If Danae missed one checkpoint, she was required to go to bed thirty minutes earlier than usual that evening. If she missed two, she hit the "lily whites" an hour before her assigned hour. She was permitted to read during that time in bed, but she could not watch television or talk on the telephone. This procedure took all the morning pressure off Shirley and placed it on our daughter's shoulders, where it belonged. There were occasions when my wife got up just in time to fix breakfast, only to find Danae sitting soberly at the piano, clothed and in her right mind.

This system of discipline can serve as a model for parents who have similar behavioral problems with their children. It was not oppressive; in fact, Danae seemed to enjoy having a target to shoot at. The limits of acceptable performance were defined beyond question. The responsibility was clearly placed on the child. And it required no adult anger or foot stamping.

There is an adaptation of this concept available to resolve other thorny conflicts in your home, too. The only limit lies in the creativity and imagination that you bring to the situation.[6]

My eight-year-old often puts his milk glass too close to his elbow when eating, and has knocked it over at least six times. I keep telling him to be careful but it just isn't within him to slow down. When he spilt the milk again yesterday, I jerked him up and gave him a spanking with a belt. Today I don't feel good about the incident. Should I have reacted more patiently?

Yes, it appears that you overreacted. Spanking should only be applied in circumstances when the *intent* of the child is to disobey or defy your authority. A table accident, even if it occurs often, does not fall in that category of rebellious behavior. Therefore, the spanking was inappropriate in the instance you described (even though I understand the frustration that caused it). It would have been better to create a method of capturing his attention and helping him remember to return his glass to a safe area. For example, you could have cut an "off limits" zone from red construction paper, and taped it to the side of his plate. If Junior placed his glass on the paper, he would have to help wash the dishes after the evening meal. I guarantee you that he would seldom "forget" again. In fact, this procedure would probably sensitize him to the location of the glass, even after the paper was removed. Again, it's important to remember that irresponsible behavior is quite different in motive than defiance and rebellion, and should be handled more creatively.[7]

My two adopted daughters are sisters. They were six and eight years old when we got them last month. They have adjusted pretty well to our home, and they respond eagerly to our love. However, they have many sloppy habits: they hadn't been taught to use a fork, so they grab food with their hands. They leave water running, won't hang up wet towels, and would never brush their teeth if I didn't stand over them. How can I teach them to take responsibility for themselves like other children their ages?

One of the most effective tools available for teaching responsibility to children involves the use of specific rewards for proper behavior. The system by which they are motivated is expressed in the "Law of Reinforcement," described by the first educational psychologist, E. L. Thorndike. It states, "Behavior which achieves desirable consequences will recur." In other words, if an individual likes what happens as a result of his behavior, he will be inclined to repeat that act. If Sally gets favorable attention from the boys on the day she wears a new dress, she will want to wear the dress again and again. If Pancho wins with one tennis racket and loses with another, he will prefer the racket with which he has found success. This principle is disarmingly simple, but it has profound implications for human learning.

My point is that a correct use of rewards (reinforcements) can make your children *want* to brush their teeth and eat with a fork and hang up wet towels. Unfortunately, it is not sufficient to dole out gifts and prizes in an unplanned manner. There are specific principles which must be followed if the Law of Reinforcement is to achieve its full potential.

Among the most important of those particulars is the need for *immediate* reinforcement. Parents often make the mistake of offering long-range rewards to children, but their successes are few. It is usually unfruitful to offer nine-year-old Joey a car when he is sixteen if he'll work hard in school during the next seven years. Second- and third-grade elementary school children are often promised a trip to Grandma's house next summer in exchange for good behavior throughout the year. Their obedience is typically unaffected by this lure. Likewise, it is unsatisfactory to offer Mary Lou a new doll for Christmas if she'll keep her room straight in July. Most children have neither the mental capacity nor the maturity to hold a long-range goal in mind day after day. Time moves slowly for them; consequently, the reinforcement seems impossible to reach and uninteresting to contemplate. For animals, a reward should be offered approximately two seconds after the behavior has occurred. A mouse will learn the turns in a maze much faster if the cheese is waiting at the end than if a five-second delay is imposed. Although children can tolerate longer delays than animals, the power of a reward is weakened with time.

Returning to the question, it is important for you to understand that the irresponsible behavior of your adopted girls has been learned. Children learn to laugh, play, run, and jump; they also learn to whine, bully, pout, fight, throw temper tantrums, or be tomboys. The universal teacher is reinforcement. The child repeats a behavior which he considers to be successful. A youngster may be cooperative and helpful because he enjoys the effect that behavior has on his parents; another will sulk and pout for the same reason. When parents recognize characteristics which they dislike in their children, they should set about *teaching* more admirable traits by allowing good behavior to succeed and bad behavior to fail.[8]

You have referred to children who manipulate their mothers and fathers. On the other hand, isn't the parent manipulating the child by the use of rewards and punishment?

No more than a factory supervisor is manipulating his employees by insisting that they arrive at work by 9:00 A.M. No more than a policeman manipulates the speeding driver by giving him a traffic ticket. No more than an insurance company manipulates that same driver by increasing his premium. The word "manipulation" implies a sinister or selfish motive. I prefer the term "leadership," which is in the best interest of everyone—even when it involves unpleasant consequences.[9]

I am uncomfortable using rewards to influence my kids. It seems too much like bribery to me. I'd like to hear your views on the subject.

Many parents feel as you do, and in response I say, don't use them if you are philosophically opposed to the concept. It is unfortunate, however, that our most workable teaching device is often rejected because of what I would consider to be a misunderstanding of terms. Our entire society is established on a system of reinforcement, yet we don't want to apply it where it is needed most: with young children. As adults, we go to work each day and receive a pay check on Friday. Getting out of bed each morning is thereby rewarded. Medals are given to brave soldiers; plaques are awarded to successful businessmen and watches are presented to retiring employees. Rewards make responsible effort worthwhile. The main reason for the overwhelming success of capitalism is that hard work and personal discipline are rewarded materially. The great weakness of socialism is the absence of reinforcement; why should a man struggle to achieve if there is nothing special to be gained? The most distasteful aspect of my brief military experience was the absence of reinforcement; I could not get a higher rank until a certain period of time had passed, no matter how hard I worked. The size of my pay check was determined by Congress, not by my competence or output. This system is a destroyer of motivation, yet some parents seem to feel it is the only way to approach children. They expect little Marvin to carry responsibility simply because it is noble for him to do so. They want him to work and learn and sweat for the sheer joy of personal discipline. He isn't going to buy it!

Consider the alternative approach to the "bribery" I've recommended. How are *you* going to get your five-year-old son to behave more responsibly? The most frequently used substitutes are nagging, complaining, begging, screaming, threatening, and punishing. The mother who objects to the use of rewards may also go to bed each evening with a headache, vowing to have no more children. She doesn't like to accentuate materialism in this manner, yet later she will be giving money to her child. Since her youngster never earns his own cash, he doesn't learn how to save it or spend it wisely or pay tithe on it. The toys she buys him are purchased with her money, and he values them less. But most important, he is not learning self-discipline and personal responsibility that is possible through the careful reinforcement of that behavior.[10]

If you don't consider the judicious use of rewards with children to be a form of bribery, then what *does* constitute an inappropriate gift?

Rewards become bribes when they serve as a "pay-off" for disobedient or irresponsible behavior. For example, it is not
recommended that rewards be utilized when the child has challenged the authority of the parent. Mom may say, "Come here,
Lucy," and Lucy shouts "No!" It is a mistake for Mom to then
offer a piece of candy if Lucy will comply with her request. She
would actually be rewarding her for defiance. Nor should
rewards be used as a substitute for authority; both reward and
punishment have a place in child management, and reversals
bring undesirable results.[11]

**I worry about putting undue emphasis on materialism
with my kids. Do rewards *have* to be in the form of money
or toys?**
Certainly not. When my daughter was three years of age, I
began to teach her some pre-reading skills, including the alpha-
bet. By planning the training sessions to occur after dinner each
evening, bits of chocolate candy provided the chief source of
motivation. (In those days I was less concerned about the effect
of excess sugar consumption than I am now.) Late one afternoon I was sitting on the floor drilling her on several new letters
when a tremendous crash shook the neighborhood. The whole
family rushed outside immediately to see what had happened,
and observed that a teenager had wrecked his car on our quiet
residential street. The boy was not badly hurt, but his automobile was a mess. We sprayed the smoldering car with water and
made the necessary phone call to the police. It was not until the
excitement began to lessen that we realized our daughter had
not followed us out of the house. I returned to the den where I
found her elbow deep in the two-pound bag of candy I had left
behind. She had put at least a pound of chocolate into her
mouth, and most of the remainder was distributed around her
chin, nose, and forehead. When she saw me coming, she managed to jam another mouthful into her chipmunk cheeks. From
this experience, I learned one of the limitations of using material, or at least edible, reinforcement.

Anything that is considered desirable to an individual can
serve as reinforcement for behavior. The most obvious rewards
for animals are those which satisfy physical needs, although
humans are further motivated to resolve their overwhelming
psychological needs. Some children, for example, would rather
receive a sincere word of praise than a ten dollar bill, particu-

larly if the adult approval is expressed in front of other children. Children and adults of all ages seek constant satisfaction of their emotional needs, including the desire for love, social acceptance, and self-respect. Additionally, they hope to find excitement, intellectual stimulation, entertainment, and pleasure.

Verbal reinforcement should permeate the entire parent-child relationship. Too often our parental instruction consists of a million "don'ts" which are jammed down the child's throat. We should spend more time rewarding him for the behavior we do admire, even if our "reward" is nothing more than a sincere compliment. Remembering the child's need for self-esteem and acceptance, the wise parent can satisfy those important longings while using them to teach valued concepts and behavior. A few examples may be helpful:

> *Mother to daughter:* You certainly colored nicely within the lines on that picture, Rene. I like to see that kind of neat art work. I'm going to put this on the bulletin board in the hall.

> *Mother to husband in son's presence:* Jack, did you notice how Don put his bicycle in the garage tonight? He used to leave it out until we told him to put it away; he is becoming much more responsible, don't you think?

> *Father to son:* I appreciate your being quiet while I was figuring the income tax, son. You were very thoughtful. Now that I have that job done, I'll have more time. Why don't we plan to go to the zoo next Saturday?

> *Teacher to high school student:* You've made a good point, Juan. I hadn't thought of that aspect of the matter. I enjoy your original way of looking at things.

> *Mother to small son:* Kevin, you haven't sucked your thumb all morning. I'm very proud of you. Let's see how long you can go this afternoon.

It is unwise for a parent to compliment the child for behavior she does not admire. If everything the child does earns him a big hug and a pat on the back, Mom's approval gradually becomes meaningless. Inflation can destroy the value of her reinforcement. Specific behavior warranting genuine compliments can be found if it is sought, even in the most immature youngster.[12]

I think I used a reward properly last Saturday night when my husband and I went out to dinner. As we were leaving, our four- and five-year-old sons set up a howl. They screamed and threw temper tantrums until I remembered how effective rewards can be. I went to the cupboard and got a sucker for each of them. Their crying stopped and we left in peace. Is this an example of using the Law of Reinforcement properly?

Unfortunately, it is not. Instead of reinforcing maturity and responsibility as you were leaving, you have inadvertently rewarded the opposite response. You see, you have made it to your children's advantage to cry the next time you plan to leave. The candy actually reinforced the tears, in this instance.

It is vitally important for parents to understand these principles, if for no other reason than to avoid rewarding unacceptable behavior. In fact, it is remarkably easy and common to propagate undesirable behavior in young children by allowing it to succeed. Suppose, for example, that Mr. and Mrs. Weakknee are having guests in for dinner tonight, and they put three-year-old Ricky to bed at 7:00 P.M. They know Ricky will cry, as he always does, but what else can they do? Indeed, Ricky cries. He begins at a low pitch (which does not succeed) and gradually builds to a high intensity scream. Finally, Mrs. Weakknee becomes so embarrassed by the display that she lets Ricky get up. What has the child learned? That he must cry loudly if he wants to get up. Mr. and Mrs. Weakknee had better be prepared for a tearful battle tomorrow night, too, because the method was successful to Ricky the night before.

Let's look at another example. Betty Sue is an argumentative teenager. She never takes "no" for an answer. She is very cantankerous; in fact, her father says the only time she is ever homesick is when she is at home. Whenever her mother is not sure about whether she wants to let Betty go to a party or ball game, she will first tell her she *can't* go. By saying an initial "no," Betty's mom doesn't commit herself to a "yes" before she's had a chance to think it over. She can always change her mind from negative to positive, but it is difficult to go the other way. However, what does this system tell Betty? She can see that "no" really means "maybe." The harder she argues and complains, the more likely she is to obtain the desired "yes." Many parents make the same mistake as Betty Sue's mother. They allow arguing, sulking, pouting, door-slamming, and bargaining to succeed. A parent should not take a definitive position on an issue until he has thought it over thoroughly. Then he should stick tenaciously to his stand. If the teenager learns that "no" means "absolutely no," he is less likely to waste his effort appealing his case to higher courts.

Perhaps a final example will be helpful: seven-year-old Abe wants the attention of his family, and he knows of no constructive way to get it. At the dinner table one evening his mother says, "Eat your beans, Abe," to which he replies defiantly, "No! I won't eat those rotten beans!" He has the eyes and ears of the whole family—something he wanted in the first place. Abe's mother can solidify the success of his defiance (and guarantee its return) by saying, "If you'll eat your beans I'll give you a treat."

Obviously, a parent must be careful in the behavior he allows to succeed. He must exercise self-discipline and patience to insure that the reinforcement which takes place is positive, not negative in its results.[13]

My four-year-old daughter, Karen, is a *whiner*. She rarely speaks in a normal voice anymore. How can I break her of this habit?

It is a well-established fact that unreinforced behavior will eventually disappear. This process, called *extinction* by psychologists, can be very useful to parents and teachers who want to alter the characteristics of children. The animal world provides many interesting examples of extinction. Consider the process by which circus elephants are taught not to throw their mighty power against the restraining chain each evening. When an elephant is young, his foot is chained to a cement block that is totally immovable. He will pull repeatedly against the barrier without success, thereby extinguishing his escape behavior. Later, a small rope and fragile stake will be sufficient to restrain the powerful elephant.

In order to eliminate an undesirable behavior, one must identify and then withhold the critical reinforcement. Let's apply this principle to the matter of whining, which you mentioned. Why does your child whine instead of speaking in a normal voice? Because you have inadvertently reinforced her whining! As long as Karen is speaking in her usual voice you are too busy to listen to her. I'm sure she babbles all day long, anyway, so you have often tuned out most of her verbiage. But when Karen speaks in a grating, irritating, obnoxious tone, you turn to see what is wrong. Karen's whining brings results; her normal voice does not; she becomes a whiner. In order to extinguish the whining, you must merely reverse the reinforcement. You should begin by saying, "I can't hear you because you're whining, Karen. I have funny ears; they just can't hear whining." After this message has been passed along for a day or two, you should show no indication of having heard a moan-tone. You should then offer immediate attention to a request made in a normal voice. If this control of reinforcement is applied properly, I guarantee it to achieve the desired results. All learning is based on this principle, and the consequences are certain and definite. Of course, Grandma and Uncle Albert may continue to reinforce the behavior you are trying to extinguish, and they can keep it alive.[14]

Isn't this system of extinction applied by the businesses that help people conquer a smoking habit or the tendency to overeat?
That's right. The objective is to eliminate the pleasantness (reinforcement) usually produced by inhaling cigarette smoke. A tube is aimed at the face of the smoker from which will come very stale, concentrated tobacco smoke. Whenever the individual takes a puff from his own cigarette, he is shot in the face with the putrid smoke from the tube. The smoker begins to associate cigarettes with the stinking, foul blast in the face, and a high percentage of cases have reported to develop a strong dislike for smoking.[15]

My child is afraid of the dark. Can the principle of extinction be helpful in overcoming this fear?
Extinction is one of the most effective tools in helping children overcome irrational fears. I consulted with a mother who was also worried about her three-year-old daughter's fear of the dark. Despite the use of a night light and leaving the bedroom door open, Marla was afraid to stay in her room alone. She insisted that her mother sit with her until she went to sleep each evening, which became very time-consuming and inconvenient. If Marla happened to awaken in the night, she would call for help. It was apparent that the child was not bluffing; she was genuinely frightened. Fears such as this are not innate characteristics in the child; they have been learned. Parents must be

very careful in expressing their fears, because their youngsters are amazingly perceptive in adopting those same concerns. For that matter, good-natured teasing can also produce problems for a child. If a youngster walks into a dark room and is pounced upon from behind the door, he has learned something from the joke: the dark is not always empty! In Marla's case, it is unclear where she learned to fear the dark, but I believe her mother inadvertently magnified the problem. In her concern for Marla, she conveyed her anxiety, and Marla began to think that her fears must be justified. "Even mother is worried about it." The fright became so great that Marla could not walk through a dimly lit room without an escort. It was at this point that the child was referred to me.

I suggested that the mother tell Marla she was going to help her see that there was nothing to be afraid of. (It is usually unfruitful to try to *talk* a child out of his fears but it helps to show him you are confident and unthreatened.) She bought a package of stars and created a chart that showed how a new phonograph player could be "earned." Then she placed her chair just outside Marla's bedroom door. Marla was offered a star if she could spend a short time (ten seconds) in her bedroom with the light on and the door open. This first step was not very threatening, and Marla enjoyed the game. It was repeated several times; then she was asked to walk a few feet into the darkened room with the door still open while Mother (clearly visible in the hall) counted to ten. Marla accomplished this task several times and was given the stars on each occasion. On subsequent trips, the door was half shut and finally closed except for the narrowest of opening. Eventually, Marla had the courage to enter the dark room, shut the door and sit on the bed while her mother counted to ten. She knew she could come out immediately if she wished. Mother talked confidently and quietly. The length of time in the dark was gradually lengthened, and instead of producing fear, it produced stars and eventually a record player; a good source of pleasure for a small child. Courage was being reinforced; fear was being extinguished. The cycle of fright was thereby broken, being replaced by a more healthy attitude.

The uses of extinction are limited only by the imagination and creativity of the parent or teacher. The best method of changing a behavior is to withhold its reinforcement while rewarding its replacement.[16]

HYPER-ACTIVITY IN CHILDREN

What is hyperactivity and what causes it?
Hyperactivity (also called hyperkinesis, minimal brain dysfunction, impulse disorder, and at least thirty other terms) is defined as excessive and *uncontrollable* movement. It usually involves distractability, restlessness, and a short attention span. I italicized the word uncontrollable because the severely affected child is absolutely incapable of sitting quietly in a chair or slowing down his level of activity. He is propelled from within by forces he can neither explain or ameliorate.

One such youngster was a seven-year-old boy named Kurt who was afflicted with Downs Syndrome (a form of mental retardation which was originally called mongolism). This little fellow was frantically active, and literally "attacked" my furniture when he entered the room. He scrambled over the top of my desk, knocking over pictures and files and paper weights. Then this lad grabbed for the telephone and held it in the direction of my ear. I humored him by faking a conversation with a mythical caller, but Kurt had other purposes in mind. He jumped from my desk and scurried into the office of a psychologist next door, insisting that my colleague play the same game. As it happened, our two phones were on the same extension, and this little seven-year-old had succeeded in outsmarting the two child development "experts." There we were, talking to each other on the phone without anything relevant to say. It was a humbling experience.

A truly hyperactive child can humble any adult, particularly if the disorder is not understood by his parent. The condition often appears related to damage to the central nervous system, although it can also be caused by emotional stress and fatigue.

Some authorities believe that virtually all children born through the birth canal (that is, not by caesarean section) are likely to sustain damage to brain tissue during the birth process. The difference between patients who are severely affected (and are called cerebral palsied) and those who have no obvious symptoms may reflect three variables: (1) Where the damage is located; (2) How massive the lesion is; and (3) How quickly it occurred. Thus, it is possible that some hyperactive children were very early afflicted by an unidentified brain interference which caused no other symptoms or problems. I must emphasize, however, that this explanation is merely speculative and that the medical understanding of this disorder is far from complete.[1]

How can damage to brain tissue cause frantic activity in a child?

Relatively little is known about the human brain and its malfunctions. I knew one neurologically impaired child, for example, who could read the words, "Go shut the door," with no understanding of the written command. However, if a tape recording was made while he read, "Go shut the door," this child could hear the replay of his own voice and understand the words perfectly. Another patient in a mental hospital could completely disassemble and repair complex television sets, yet did not have the common sense to handle the routine responsibilities of living outside a hospital setting. Another man, wounded in combat, had the sad characteristic of being unable to keep any thought to himself. He mumbled his innermost ideas, to the embarrassment and shock of everyone nearby.

Brain disorders are expressed in many strange ways, including the frenzy of hyperactivity. No one can explain exactly why it happens, other than the obvious fact that the electrochemical mechanisms which control body movement have been altered, resulting in excessive stimulation to the muscles.[2]

How can anxiety or emotional problems cause hyperactivity?

When adults are under severe stress or anxiety, their inner tension is typically expressed in the form of physical activity. An expectant father "paces the floor," or smokes one cigarette after another, or his hands may tremble. A basketball coach will race up and down the sidelines while the outcome of the game is in doubt. Another anxious person may sit quietly in a chair, but his fingernails will be chewed to the quick or he will move his lower jaw slowly from side to side. My point is that tension increases the amount of bodily movement observed in adults.

How much more true that is of an immature child. He doesn't merely drum his fingers on a table when he is anxious; he tries to climb the curtains and walk on the ceiling.[3]

How early can the problem be identified?
The severely hyperactive child can be recognized during early toddlerhood. In fact, he can't be ignored. By the time he is thirty months of age he may have exhausted his mother, irritated his siblings, and caused the grandparents to retire from baby-sitting duties. No family member is "uninvolved" with his problem. Instead of growing out of it, as the physician may promise, he continues to attack his world with the objective of disassembling it (at least until puberty).[4]

Is there a "normal" hyperactivity?
Certainly. Not every child who squirms, churns, and bounces is technically "hyperactive." Most toddlers are "on the move" from dawn to dark (as are their mothers).[5]

Then how can I tell whether my child is just normally active or genuinely hyperactive? And how can I decipher whether his problem is the result of emotional or a physical impairment?
These questions are difficult to answer, and few parents have the training to resolve them. Your best resource in evaluating your child's problem is your pediatrician or family physician. Even he may have to guess at a diagnosis and its cause. He can, however, make a complete medical evaluation and then refer you, if necessary, to other professionals for specific assistance. Your child may require the services of a remedial reading teacher or a speech and hearing therapist or a psychologist who can assess intellectual and perceptual abilities and offer management advice. You should not try alone to cope with an excessively active child if this additional support and consultation is available.[6]

What role does nutrition play?

The role of nutrition in hyperactivity is a very controversial issue which I am not qualified to resolve; I can only offer my opinion on the subject. American people have been told that hyperactivity is a product of red food coloring, too much sugar intake, inadequate vitamins, and many related causes resulting from poor nutrition. I don't doubt for a moment that improper eating habits have the capacity to destroy us physically and could easily be related to the phenomenon of hyperactivity. However, I am of the opinion that the writers of many faddish books on this subject are trying to make their guesses sound like proven facts. Many of the answers are not yet available, which explains why so many "authorities" disagree violently among themselves.

The nutritionists whom I respect most highly are those who take a cautious, scientific approach to these complex questions. I am suspicious of the self-appointed experts who bypass their own professional publications and come directly to the lay public with unsupported conclusions which even their colleagues reject.

The above paragraph may irritate some parents who are following the advice of a lone-wolf nutritional writer. To those readers I can only say, "Do what succeeds." If your child is more calm and sedate when avoiding certain foods, then use your judgment as you continue the successful dietary regimen. Your opinion is probably as valid as mine.[7]

How common is hyperactivity?

Authorities disagree on the incidence of hyperactivity, but this disorder apparently afflicts between 6 and 10 percent of all children under ten years of age. Males outnumber females four to one.[8]

There are times when I strongly resent my hyperactive child. Do other mothers share this frustration?

Your response is typical. Every mother of a hyperactive child occasionally experiences a distressing tug-of-war in her mind. On the one side, she understands her child's problem and feels a deep empathy and love for her little fellow. There is nothing that she wouldn't do to help him. But on the other side, she resents the chaos he has brought into her life. Speedy Gonzales spills his milk and breaks vases and teeters on the brink of disaster throughout the day. He embarrasses his mother in public and shows little appreciation for the sacrifices she is making on his behalf. By the time bedtime arrives, she often feels as if she has spent the entire day in a foxhole.

What happens, then, when genuine love and strong resentment collide in the mind of a mother or father? The inevitable result is parental guilt in sizeable proportions—guilt that is terribly destructive to a woman's peace of mind and even to her health.[9]

What other problems does the hyperactive child face?

The child with exaggerated activity usually experiences three specific difficulties in addition to his frantic motion. First, he is likely to develop psychological problems resulting from rejection by his peers. His nervous energy is not only irritating to adults, but tends to drive away friends as well. He may be branded as a troublemaker and goof-off in the classroom. Furthermore, his emotional response is often unstable, swinging unpredictably from laughter to tears in a matter of moments, and causing his peers to think him strange. In short, the hyperactive child can easily fall victim to feelings of inferiority and the emotional upheaval which is inevitably generated by rejection and low self-esteem.

Second, the active child frequently experiences severe learning problems during the school years. He finds it difficult, if not impossible, to remain in his seat and concentrate on his lessons. His attention span is miniscule throughout elementary school, which leads to mischievousness and distractability while his teachers are speaking. He never seems to know what the educational program is all about, and his frustrated teachers often describe him as being "in a fog."

But there is another academic difficulty which is also extremely common among hyperactive children: visual-perceptual problems. A child may have perfectly normal vision, yet not "perceive" symbols and printed material accurately. In other words, his eyes may be perfect but his brain does not process the signal properly. Such a child may "see" letters and numbers reversed or distorted. It is particularly difficult for him to learn to read or write.

Reading is a highly complex neurological skill. It requires the recognition of symbols and their transmittal to the brain, where

they must be interpreted, remembered, and (perhaps) spoken as
a language. Any break in this functional chain will inhibit the
final product. Furthermore, this process must occur rapidly
enough to permit a steady flow of ideas from the written materials. Many hyperactive children simply do not have the
neurological apparatus to develop these skills and are destined
to experience failure during the primary grades in school.[10]

What are the solutions?

There are dozens of medications which have been shown to be
effective in calming the hyperactive child. Since every child's
chemistry is unique, it may be necessary for a physician to
"fish" for the right substance and dosage. Let me stress that I
am opposed to the administration of such drugs to children who
do not require them. In some instances these substances have
been given indiscriminately to children simply because their
parents or teachers preferred them sedated, which is inexcus-
able. Every medication has an undesirable side effect (even
aspirin) and should be administered only after careful evaluation and study. However, if your child displays extreme
symptoms of hyperactivity and has been evaluated by a neurologist or other knowledgeable physician, you should not hesitate
to accept his prescription of an appropriate medication. Some
dramatic behavioral changes can occur when the proper substance is identified for a particular child.[11]

But won't the long-term use of medication increase the possibility of my child becoming a drug user during adolescence?

Most authorities feel that the use of medication in childhood
does not necessarily lead to drug abuse in later life. In fact,
a federal task force was appointed in 1971 to consider that
possibility. The conclusion from their investigation emphasized
the appropriateness of medications in treatment of hyperactive
children. Some children need, and should get, the proper calming agent.[12]

Do medications solve all the problems?

Usually not. Let's consider the three primary symptoms as
related to medications:

1. Hyperactivity. The proper prescription can be very effective in "normalizing" a child's motor activity. Treatment is most successful in controlling this symptom.

2. Psychological difficulties. Medication is less effective in eliminating emotional problems. Once a child has been "slowed down," the process of building his self-image and social acceptance must begin in earnest. The administration of drugs may make the objective possible, but it does not, in itself, eradicate the problem.

3. Visual-perceptual problems. Drug usage is of no value in resolving neurological malfunctions which interfere with perception. There are training materials available which have been shown to be helpful, including those provided by the Marianne Frostig Center for Educational Therapy. Dr. Frostig is a pioneer in the field of learning disabilities, and has provided books, films, and evaluative tests for use by teachers and trained professionals. Your local school district can obtain a list of available resources by contacting this organization at 5981 Venice Boulevard, Los Angeles, California 90034. Many school districts also provide special classes for children with unique learning disabilities, which can be of inestimable value to a handicapped student.

It is obvious that drug therapy cannot provide the total remedy. A pharmaceutical approach must be combined with parental adaptations and educational alternatives, among others.[13]

How does the parent "discipline" a hyperactive child?
It is often assumed that an excessively active child should be indulged, simply because he has a physical problem. I couldn't disagree more. Every youngster needs the security of defined limits, and the hyperactive boy or girl is no exception. Such a child should be held responsible for his behavior, like the rest of the family. Of course, your level of expectation must be adjusted to fit his limitations. For example, most children can be required to sit in a chair for disciplinary reasons, whereas the hyperactive child would not be able to remain there.
Similarly, spankings are sometimes ineffective with a highly excitable little bundle of electricity. As with every aspect of parenthood, disciplinary measures for the hyperactive child must be suited to his unique characteristics and needs.

How, then, is the child to be controlled? What advice is available for the parents of a child with this problem? Listed below are eighteen helpful suggestions quoted from a very helpful book entitled *The Hyperactive Child,* by Dr. Domeena Renshaw.[14]

1. Be carefully consistent in rules and disciplines.
2. Keep your own voice quiet and slow. Anger is normal. Anger can be controlled. Anger does not mean you do not love a child.
3. Try hard to keep your emotions cool by bracing for expectable turmoil. Recognize and respond to any positive behavior, however small. If you search for good things, you will find a few.
4. Avoid a ceaselessly negative approach: "Stop"— "Don't"—"No"—
5. Separate behavior which you may not like, from the child's person, which you like, e.g., "I like you. I don't like your tracking mud through the house."
6. Have a very clear routine for this child. Construct a timetable for waking, eating, play, TV, study, chores, and bedtime. Follow it flexibly although he disrupts it. Slowly your structure will reassure him until he develops his own.
7. Demonstrate new or difficult tasks, using action accompanied by short, clear, quiet explanations. Repeat the demonstration until learned. This uses audio-visual-sensory perceptions to reinforce the learning. The memory traces of a hyperkinetic child take longer to form. Be patient and repeat.
8. Try a separate room or a part of a room which is his own special area. Avoid brilliant colors or complex patterns in decor. Simplicity, solid colors, minimal clutter, and a worktable facing a blank wall away from distractions assist concentration. A hyperkinetic child cannot "filter" out overstimulation himself yet.
9. Do one thing at a time: give him one toy from a closed box; clear the table of everything else when coloring; turn off the radio/TV when he is doing homework. Multiple stimuli prevent his concentration from focusing on his primary task.
10. Give him responsibility, which is essential for growth. The task should be within his capacity, although the assignment may need much supervision. Acceptance

and recognition of his efforts (even when imperfect) should not be forgotten.

11. Read his preexplosive warning signals. Quietly intervene to avoid explosions by distracting him or discussing the conflict calmly. Removal from the battle zone to the sanctuary of his room for a few minutes is useful.

12. Restrict playmates to one or at most two at one time, because he is so excitable. Your home is more suitable, so you can provide structure and supervision. Explain your rules to the playmate and briefly tell the other parent your reasons.

13. Do not pity, tease, be frightened by, or overindulge this child. He has a special condition of the nervous system which is manageable.

14. Know the name and dose of his medication. Give these regularly. Watch and remember the effects to report back to your physician.

15. Openly discuss any fears you have about the use of medications with your physician.

16. Lock up all medications, including these, to avoid accidental misuse.

17. Always supervise the taking of medication, even if it is routine over a long period of years. Responsibility remains with the parents! One day's supply at a time can be put in a regular place and checked routinely as he becomes older and more self-reliant.

18. Share your successful "helps" with his teacher. The outlined ways to help your hyperkinetic child are as important to him as diet and insulin are to a diabetic child.[15]

What does the future hold?

In case you haven't heard, help is on the way. The maturation and glandular changes associated with puberty often calm the hyperactive youngster between twelve and eighteen years of age. This explains why we seldom see adults jumping from the backs of chairs and rolling on the floor. But for harassed parents who spend their days chasing a nonstop toddler around the house, there may be little consolation in knowing that the crisis will last only nine more years.

Note: For parents who want to learn more about children with hyperactivity, I would refer them to Dr. Renshaw's excellent book. While the writing style is somewhat technical, it is certainly readable and contains helpful insights. See footnote 14 for publication details.[16]

COPING WITH ADOLESCENCE

I know it is my responsibility to teach Ricky, my preteenager, the essentials of reproduction and sex education before he reaches adolescence. But what else should I tell him?

He must be told, among other things, about the dramatic physical changes that are about to occur within his body. I have found that uninformed teenagers fall into two broad categories: The first group doesn't know these changes are coming and are worried sick by what they see happening. The second group is aware that certain features are supposed to appear and are anxious because the changes are late in arriving. That's why doubts and fears are so common during the adolescent years. Yet, they can be avoided by healthy, confident parental instruction before the fears develop.[1]

Please be more specific. What are the major physical changes which I should tell Ricky about?

There are four topics that are "musts" for a conversation of this nature. Let me present them briefly.

1. Rapid growth will occur, sapping energy and strength for a while. The teenager will actually need more sleep and better nutrition than when he was younger.

2. Tell your child that his body will quickly change to that of an adult. His sex organs will become more mature and will be surrounded by pubic hair. (For males, stress this point: the size of the penis is of no physical importance. Many boys worry about having a smaller organ, but that has *nothing* to do with fathering a child or sexual satisfaction as an adult. For your

daughter, breast development should also be discussed in the same manner.)

3. The full details of the menstrual cycle must be made clear to your girl before her first period. It is a terrifying thing for a girl to experience this aspect of maturity without forewarning. Many books and films are available to help explain this developmental milestone, and should be used. The most important parental responsibility at this point is to convey confidence, optimism, and excitement regarding menstruation, rather than saying sadly, "This is the cross you must bear as a woman."

4. It is most important that the timing of puberty be discussed with your children, for herein lies *much* grief and distress. This period of heightened sexual development may occur as early as twelve or as late as nineteen years of age in boys and from ten to seventeen in girls. Thus, it may arrive seven years earlier in some children than in others! And the youngsters who develop very early or very late usually face some upsetting psychological problems. There are four extremes which should be considered:

The Late-Maturing Boy. This little fellow knows perfectly well that he is still a baby while his friends have grown up. He picks up the telephone and the operator calls him "Ma'am"! What an insult! He's very interested in athletics at this age, but he can't compete with the larger, stronger boys. He gets teased in the locker room about his sexual immaturity, and his self-esteem nosedives. And adding insult to injury, he is actually shorter than most of the girls for a couple of years! (They have had their growth spurt and he has not.) He fears that there is something drastically wrong in his case, but he dares not mention his thoughts to anyone. It's too embarrassing. The prepubertal child can often be the worst troublemaker in the school, for he has many things to prove about his doubtful manhood.

The Late Maturing Girl. Life is no easier for the girl whose internal clock is on the slow side. She looks down at her flat chest and then glances at her busty friends. For two or three years, her girl friends have been sharing confidences about menstruation, but she can't participate in the discussions. She has been nicknamed "baby face" by the gang, and in fact, she does look about eight years old. Remembering the role physical attractiveness plays in self-esteem, the reader can see that inferiority can overwhelm the late developer, even if he or she *is*

attractively arranged. And unless someone tells them otherwise, they are likely to conclude that they will never grow up.

The Early Maturing Girl. If it is disadvantageous to be late in
maturing, one would think that the opposite would be
emotionally healthy. Not so. Since girls tend to develop sexually
one or two years before boys, on an average, the girl who enters
puberty before other girls is miles ahead of everybody else her
age. Physical strength offers her no real advantages in our
society, and it is simply not acceptable to be boy-crazy at ten
years of age. For two or three uncomfortable years, the early
maturing girl is out of step with all her age mates.

The Early Maturing Boy. By contrast, the early maturing boy is
blessed with a great social advantage. He is strong at a time
when power is worshiped by his peers, and his confidence soars
as his athletic successes are publicized. His early development
places him on a par with the girls in his class, who are also
awakening sexually. Thus, he has the field all to himself for a
year or two. Research confirms that the early maturing boy is
more frequently emotionally stable, confident, and socially
accepted than other boys. It also shows that he is more likely to
be more successful in later adult life, as well.

   In the discussion of these extremes with your preteenager,
assure him that it is "normal" for some youngsters to be early or
late in developing. It does not mean that anything is wrong with
his body. If indeed your child is a late bloomer, he will need
additional reassurance and encouragement at the time of this
conversation to open the door of communication regarding the
fears and anxieties associated with physical growth and
development.[2]

**My thirteen-year-old son has become increasingly lazy in
the past couple of years. He lies around the house and will
sleep half a day on Saturday. He complains about being
tired a lot. Is this typical of early adolescence? How
should I deal with it?**
It is not uncommon for boys and girls to experience fatigue
during the pubertal years. Their physical resources are being
invested in a rapid growth process during that time, leaving less
energy for other activities. This period doesn't last very long
and is usually followed by the most energetic time of life.

I would suggest, first, that you take your son for a routine physical examination to rule out the possibility of a more serious explanation for his fatigue. If it does turn out to be a phenomenon of puberty, as I suspect, you should "go with the flow." See that he gets plenty of rest and sleep. This need is often not met, however, because teenagers feel that they should not have to go to bed as early as they did when they were children. Therefore, they stay up too late and then drag through the next day in a state of exhaustion. Surprisingly, a twelve- or thirteen-year-old person actually needs more rest than when he was nine or ten, simply because of the acceleration in growth.

What I'm saying is that you should let your son sleep on Saturday morning, if possible. It is often difficult for mothers and fathers to permit their overgrown son or daughter to lie in bed until 9:30 A.M., when the grass needs mowing. However, they should know that he is lying in bed because he needs more sleep, and they would be wise to let him get it. *Then* ask him to mow the lawn when he awakens.

Second, the foods your son eats are also very important during this time. His body needs the raw materials with which to construct new muscle cells, bones, and fibers that are in the plans. Hot dogs, donuts, and milkshakes just won't do the job. Again, it is even more important to eat a *balanced* diet during this time.

In summary, your son is turning overnight from a boy to a man. Some of the physical characteristics you are observing are part of that transformation. Do everything you can to facilitate it.[3]

My thirteen-year-old daughter is still built like a boy, but she is insisting that her mother buy her a bra. Believe me, she has no need for it, and the only reason she wants one is because most of her friends do. Should I give in?
Your straight and narrow daughter needs a bra to be like her friends, to compete, to avoid ridicule, and to feel like a woman. Those are excellent reasons. Your wife should meet this request by tomorrow morning, if not sooner.[4]

Our teenage daughter has become extremely modest in recent months, demanding that even her sisters leave her room when she's dressing. I think this is silly, don't you?

No, I would suggest that you honor her requests for privacy. Her sensitivity is probably caused by an awareness that her body is changing, and she is embarrassed by recent developments (or the lack of them). This is likely to be a temporary phase and you should not oppose her in it.[5]

Children seem to be growing up at a younger age today than in the past. Is this true, and if so, what accounts for their faster development?

Yes, it *is* true. Statistical records indicate that our children are growing taller today than in the past, probably resulting from better nutrition, medicine, exercise, rest and recreation. And this more ideal physical environment has apparently caused sexual maturity to occur at younger and younger ages. It is thought that puberty in a particular child is "turned on" when he reaches a certain level of growth; therefore, when environmental circumstances propel him upward at a faster rate, he becomes sexually mature much earlier. For example, in 1850, the average age of menarche (first menstruation) in Norwegian girls was 17.0 years of age; in 1950, it was 13.0. The average age of puberty had dropped four years in that one century. In the United States the average age of the menarche dropped from 14.2 in 1900 to 12.9 in 1950. More recent figures indicate the average has now dropped closer to 12.6 years of age! Thus, the trend toward younger dating and sexual awareness is a result, at least in part, of this physiological mechanism. I suppose we could slow it down by taking poorer care of our children . . . but I doubt if that idea will gain much support.[6]

I am hurt because my teenager seems to be ashamed to be seen with me. I gave birth to him and have nourished and devoted my entire life to him. Now he's suddenly embarrassed to be seen with me, especially when his friends are around. Is this normal? Should I resist or accept it?

You should understand that teenagers are engulfed by a tremendous desire to be adults, and they resent anything which implies that they are still children. When they are seen with "Mommie and Daddy" on a Friday night, for example, their humiliation is almost unbearable. They are not really ashamed of their parents; they are embarrassed by the adult-baby role that was more appropriate in prior years. Though it is difficult for you now, you would do well to accept this healthy aspect of growing up without becoming defensive about it. Your love relationship with your child will be reestablished in a few years, although it will never be a parent-child phenomenon again. And that's the way God designed the process to work.[7]

Must I act like a teenager myself in dress, language, tastes, and manner in order to show my adolescent that I understand him?

No. There is something disgusting about a thirty-five-year-old "adolescent has-been." It wasn't necessary for you to crawl on the floor and throw temper tantrums in order to understand your two-year-old; likewise, you can reveal an empathy and acceptance of the teen years without becoming an anachronistic teenybopper yourself. In fact, the very reason for your adolescent's unique manner and style is to display an identity separate from yours. You'll turn him off quickly by invading his territory, leading him to conclude, "Mom tries so hard, but I wish she'd grow up!" Besides, he will still need an authority figure on occasion, and you've got the job![8]

How can I teach my fourteen-year-old the value of money?

One good technique is to give him enough cash to meet a particular need, and then let him manage it. You can begin by offering a weekly food allowance to be spent in school. If he squanders the total on a weekend date, then it becomes his responsibility to either work for his lunches or go hungry. This is the cold reality he will face in later life, and it will not harm him to experience the lesson while still an adolescent.

I should indicate that this principle has been known to backfire, occasionally. A physician friend of mine has four daughters and he provides each one with an annual clothing allowance when they turn twelve years of age. It then becomes the girls' responsibility to budget their money for the garments that will be needed throughout the year. The last child to turn twelve, however, was not quite mature enough to handle the assignment. She celebrated her twelfth birthday by buying an expensive coat, which cut deeply into her available capital. The following spring, she exhausted her funds totally and wore shredded stockings, holey panties, and frayed dresses for the last three months of the year. It was difficult for her parents not to intervene, but they had the courage to let her learn this valuable lesson about money management.

Perhaps your son has never learned the value of money because it comes too easily. Anything in abundant supply becomes rather valueless. I would suggest that you restrict the pipeline and maximize the responsibility required in all expenditures.[9]

What is the most difficult period of adolescence, and what is behind the distress?

The thirteenth and fourteenth years commonly are the most difficult twenty-four months in life. It is during this time that self-doubt and feelings of inferiority reach an all-time high, amidst the greatest social pressures yet experienced. An adolescent's worth as a human being hangs precariously on peer group acceptance, which can be tough to garner. Thus, relatively minor evidences of rejection or ridicule are of major significance to those who already see themselves as fools and failures. It is difficult to overestimate the impact of having no one to sit with on the school-sponsored bus trip, or of not being invited to an important event, or of being laughed at by the "in" group, or of waking up in the morning to find seven shiny new pimples on your bumpy forehead, or of being slapped by the girl you thought had liked you as much as you liked her. Some boys and girls consistently face this kind of social catastrophe throughout their teen years. They will never forget the experience.

Dr. Urie Bronfenbrenner, eminent authority on child development at Cornell University, told a Senate committee that the junior high years are probably the most critical to the development of a child's mental health. It is during this period of self-doubt that the personality is often assaulted and damaged beyond repair. Consequently, said Bronfenbrenner, it is not unusual for healthy, happy children to enter junior high school, but then emerge two years later as broken, discouraged teenagers.

I couldn't agree more emphatically with Bronfenbrenner's opinion at this point. Junior high school students are typically brutal to one another, attacking and slashing a weak victim in much the same way a pack of northern wolves kill and devour a deformed caribou. Few events stir my righteous indignation more than seeing a vulnerable child—fresh from the hand of the Creator in the morning of his life—being taught to hate himself and despise his physical body and wish he had never been born.[10]

Nothing is so distressing to me as when I see my son suffering from low self-esteem. He is in junior high now, and I know he's going through a tough time. Can you assure me that he'll come out of this difficult phase? Or is it going to mess up his life for years to come?

Despite all that I have written about the heartache of low self-esteem, there is a positive side of the matter which will encourage you. Remember that the human personality grows through mild adversity, *provided it is not crushed in the process.* Contrary to what you might believe, the ideal environment for your child is not one devoid of problems and trials. I would not, even if I could, sweep aside every hurdle from the paths of my children, leaving them to glide along in mirth. They deserve the right to face problems and profit from the confrontation.

I have verified the value of minor stress from my own experience. My childhood was remarkably happy and carefree. I was loved beyond any doubt, and my academic performance was never a cause for discomfort. In fact, I have enjoyed happiness and fulfillment thus far my entire lifetime, with the exception of two painful years. Those stressful years occurred during my seventh- and eighth-grade days, lasting through ages thirteen and fourteen.

During this period of time, I found myself in a social crossfire, giving rise to the same intense feelings of inferiority and self-doubt I have described herein. As strange as it seems, however, these two years have contributed more positive features to my adult personality than any other span of which I am aware. My empathy for others, my desire to succeed in life, my motivation in graduate school, my understanding of inferiority, and my communication with teenagers are primarily the products of an agitated adolescence. Who would have thought anything useful could have come from those twenty-four months? Yet the discomfort proved to be a valuable instructor in this instance.

Though it is hard to accept at the time, your child also needs the minor setbacks and disappointments which come his way. How can he learn to cope with problems and frustration if his early experiences are totally without trial? A tree which is planted in a rain forest is never forced to extend its roots downward in search of water; consequently it remains poorly anchored and can be toppled by a moderate wind storm. But a mesquite tree planted in a dry desert is threatened by its hostile environment. It can only survive by sending its roots more than thirty feet deep into the earth, seeking cool water. Through its adaptation to the arid land, something else happens. The well-rooted tree becomes strong and steady against all assailants.

This illustration applies to our children, as well: those who have learned to conquer their problems are more secure than those who have never faced them. Our task as parents, then, is not to eliminate every challenge for our children; it is to serve as a confident ally on their behalf, encouraging when they are distressed, intervening when the threats are overwhelming, and above all, giving them the tools with which to overcome the obstacles.[11]

Our fifteen-year-old son literally seethes with hostility at home—at his mother and me—at his sisters—at the world. Believe me, we have done nothing to provoke this anger and I don't understand what has caused it. But other parents of teens report the same problem. Why are so many adolescents angry at their parents and family? Sometimes they seem to hate the people who love them the most!

At least part of the answer to that question can be explained by the "in-between" status of teenagers. They live in an era when they enjoy neither the privileges of adulthood nor the advantages of childhood. Consider the plight of the average fifteen-year-old. All of the highly advertised adult privileges and vices are forbidden to him because he is "too young." He can't drive or marry or enlist or drink or smoke or work or leave home. And his sexual desires are denied gratification at a time when they scream for release. The only thing he is permitted to do, it seems, is stay in school and read his dreary textbooks. This is an overstatement, of course, but it is expressed from the

viewpoint of the young man or woman who feels disenfran-
chised and insulted by society. Much of the anger of today's
youth is generated by their perception of this injustice.

There is another side to this issue of adolescent volatility. I'm
now convinced that the hormonal changes occurring in a
developing body may be more important to feelings than we
thought earlier. Just as emotions are set on edge by pre-
menstrual tension, menopause, and extreme fatigue, it is
entirely possible that the adolescent experience is largely
hormonal as well. How else can we explain the *universality* of
emotional instability during these years? Having watched
thousands of children sail from childhood to early adolescence,
it still amazes me to witness textbook characteristics suddenly
appearing on schedule as though responding to a pre-
programmed computer. In fact, they probably are. I can't prove
this hypothesis to be valid, but it is making more sense to me
year by year.

**All right, so my kid feels disrespected and hostile. I still
have to impose some limits and discipline on him, don't I?**
Yes, but it is possible to lead teenagers without insulting and
antagonizing them unnecessarily. I learned this lesson when I
was a junior high school teacher. It became clear to me very
early that I could impose all manner of discipline and strict
behavioral requirements on my students, *provided* I treated
each young person with genuine dignity and respect. I earned
their friendship before and after school, during lunch, and
through classroom encounters. I was tough, especially when
challenged, but never discourteous, mean, or insulting. I
defended the underdog and tenaciously tried to build each
child's confidence and self-respect. However, I never
compromised my standards of deportment. Students entered
my classroom without talking each day. They did not chew
gum, behave disrespectfully, curse, or stab one another with
ball point pens. I was clearly the captain of the ship and I
directed it with military zeal.

The result of this combination of kindness and firm discipline
stands as one of the most pleasant memories of my professional
life. I *loved* my students and had every reason to believe that I
was loved in return. I actually missed them on weekends (a fact
my wife never quite understood). At the end of the final year
when I was packing my books and saying good-bye, there were

twenty-five or thirty teary-eyed kids who hung around my
gloomy room for several hours and finally stood sobbing in the
parking lot as I drove away. And yes, I shed a few tears of my
own that day. (Please forgive this self-congratulatory paragraph.
I haven't bothered to tell you about my failures, which are far
less interesting.)[12]

**My teenage son rarely mixes with his peers and is
involved in very few activities. He just wants to stay in
his room most of the time, and rarely even talks on the
telephone. What do you think causes him to isolate
himself in this way?**
He may have adopted one of the most common ways of dealing
with deep feelings of inadequacy and inferiority, which is to
surrender and withdraw. The individual who chooses this
approach has concluded in his own mind that he *is* inferior. He
measures his worth by the reaction of his peers, which can be
devastating during the competitive adolescent years. Thus, he
concludes, "Yes, it's true! I am a failure, just as I feared. Even
now people are laughing at me. Where can I hide?"

Having accepted his own unworthiness, which was his first
mistake, he is forced to guard his wounded ego from further
damage. "Caution" becomes his watchword. He withdraws into
a shell of silence and loneliness, choosing to take no chances nor
assume any unnecessary emotional risks.

Especially during the elementary school years, I believe we
have much greater reason to be concerned about the emotional
health of the withdrawing child than we do the more aggressive
troublemaker. Children at both extremes often need adult
intervention, but the surrenderer is much less likely to get it. He
doesn't bug anybody. He cooperates with his teacher and tries to
avoid conflict with his peers. But his quiet manner is
dangerously misleading. The adults in his life may fail to notice
that his destructive self-image is rapidly solidifying and will
never be pliable again. Considering all the alternative ways to
cope with inferiority, withdrawal is probably the least effective
and most painful.

Knowing what your son is feeling, you should have a greater
understanding of what he needs from you in the way of love and
support.[13]

My son, Brian, is now fourteen years old and he has suddenly entered a period of rebellion like nothing I've ever seen. He is breaking rules right and left and he seems to hate the entire family. He becomes angry when his mother and I try to discipline him, of course, but even during more tranquil times he seems to resent us for merely being there. Last Friday night he arrived home an hour beyond his deadline, but refused to explain why he was late or make apologetic noises. We are in the midst of a nightmare I *never* anticipated when he was younger.

This is my question. I would like you to tell me exactly how to approach this situation, even roleplaying my task of confronting him. I need to know what to say when that moment arrives.

Certainly. I would recommend that you invite Brian out to breakfast on a Saturday morning, leaving the rest of the family at home. It would be best if this event could occur during a relatively tranquil time, certainly not in the midst of a hassle or intergenerational battle. Admit that you have some important matters to discuss with him which can't be communicated adequately at home, but don't "tip your hand" before Saturday morning. Then at the appropriate moment during breakfast convey the following messages (or an adaptation thereof):

A. Brian, I wanted to talk to you this morning because of the changes that are taking place in you and in our home. We both know that the past few weeks have not been very pleasant. You have been angry most of the time and have become disobedient and rude. And your mother and I haven't done so well either. We've become irritable and we've said things that we've regretted later. This is not what God wants of us as parents, or of you as our son. There has to be a more creative way of solving our problems. That's why we're all here.

B. As a place to begin, Brian, I want you to understand what is happening. You have gone into a new period of life known as adolescence. This is the final phase of childhood, and it is often a very stormy and difficult few years. Nearly everyone on earth goes through these rough years during their early teens, and you are right on schedule at this moment. Many of the problems you face today were predictable from the day you were born, simply because growing up has never been an easy thing to do. There are even greater pressures on kids today than when we were young. I've said that to tell you this: we understand you and love you as much as we ever did, even though the past few months have been difficult in our home.

C. What is actually taking place, you see, is that you have had a taste of freedom. You are tired of being a little boy who was told what to wear and when to go to bed and what to eat. That is a healthy attitude which will help you grow up. However, now you want to be your own boss and make your own decisions without interference from anyone. Brian, you will get what you want in a very short time. You are fourteen now, and you'll soon be fifteen and seventeen and nineteen. You will be grown in a twinkling of an eye, and we will no longer have any responsibility for you. The day is coming when you will marry whomever you wish, go to whatever school you choose, select the profession or job that suits you. Your mother and I will not try to make those decisions for you. We will respect your adulthood. Furthermore, Brian, the closer you get to those days, the more freedom we plan to give you. You have more privileges now than you had last year, and that trend will continue. We will soon set you free, and you will be accountable only to God and yourself.

D. But, Brian, you must understand this message: you are not grown yet. During the past few weeks, you have wanted your mother and me to leave you alone—to let you stay out half the night if you chose—to fail in school—to carry no responsibility at home. And you have "blown up" whenever we have denied even your most extreme demands. The truth of the matter is, you have wanted us to grant you twenty-year-old freedom during the fourteenth year, although you still expect to have your shirts ironed and your meals fixed and your bills paid. You have wanted the best of both worlds with none of the responsibilities. So what are we to do? The easiest thing would be for us to let you have your way. There would be no hassles and no conflict and no more frustration. Many parents of fourteen-year-old sons and daughters have done just that. But we must not yield to this temptation. You are not ready for that complete independence, and we would be showing hatred for you (instead of love) if we surrendered at this time. We would regret our mistake for the rest of our lives, and you would soon blame us, too. And as you know, you have two younger sisters who are watching you very closely, and must be protected from the things you are teaching them.

E. Besides, Brian, God has given us a responsibility as parents to do what is right for you, and He is holding us accountable for the way we do that job. I want to read you an important passage from the Bible which describes a father named Eli who did not discipline and correct his two unruly teenage sons. (Read the dramatic story from *The Living Bible*, 1 Samuel 2:12-17, 22-25, 27-34; 3:11-14; 4:1-3 and 10-22.) It is very clear that God was angry at Eli for permitting his sons to be disrespectful and disobedient. Not only did He allow the sons to be killed in battle, but He also punished their father for not accepting his parental responsibilities. This assignment to parents can be found throughout the Bible: mothers and fathers are expected to train their children and discipline them when required. What I'm saying is that God will not hold us blameless if we let you behave in ways that are harmful to yourself and others.

F. That brings us to the question of where we go from this moment. I want to make a pledge to you, here and now: your mother and I intend to be more sensitive to your needs and feelings than we've been in the past. We're not perfect, as you well know, and it is possible that you will feel we have been unfair at one time or another. If that occurs, you can express your views and we will listen to you. We want to keep the door of communication standing wide open between us. When you seek a new privilege, I'm going to ask myself this question, "Is there any way I can grant this request without harming Brian or other people?" If I can permit what you want in good conscience, I will do so. I will compromise and bend as far as my best judgment will let me.

G. But hear this, Brian. There will be a few matters that cannot be compromised. There will be occasions when I will have to say "no." And when those times come, you can expect me to stand like the Rock of Gibraltar. No amount of violence and temper tantrums and door slamming will change a thing. In fact, if you choose to fight me in those remaining rules, then I promise that you will lose dramatically. Admittedly you're too big and grown up to spank, but I can still make you uncomfortable. And that will be my goal. Believe me, Brian, I'll lie awake nights figuring how to make you miserable. I have the courage and the determination to do my job during these last few years you are at home, and I intend to use all of my resources for this purpose, if necessary. So it's up to you. We can have a peaceful time of cooperation at home, or we can spend this last part of your childhood in unpleasantness and struggle. Either way, you *will* arrive home when you are told, and you *will* carry your share of responsibility in the family and you *will* continue to respect your mother and me.

H. Finally, Brian, let me emphasize the message I gave you in the beginning. We love you more than you can imagine, and we're going to remain friends during this difficult time. There is so much pain in the world today. Life involves disappointment and loss and rejection and aging and sickness and ultimately death. You haven't felt much of that discomfort yet, but you'll taste it soon enough. So with all that heartache outside our door, let's not bring more of it on ourselves. We need each other. We need you, and believe it or not, you still need us occasionally. And that, I suppose, is what we wanted to convey to you this morning. Let's make it better from now on.

I. Do you have things that need to be said to us?

The content of this message should be modified to fit individual circumstances and the needs of particular adolescents. Furthermore, the responses of children will vary tremendously from person to person. An "open" boy or girl may reveal his deepest feelings at such a moment of communication, permitting a priceless time of catharsis and ventilation. On the other hand, a stubborn, defiant, proud adolescent may sit immobile with head downward. But even if your teenager remains stoic or hostile, at least the cards have been laid on the table and parental intentions explained.[14]

You stated earlier that you do not favor spanking a teenager. What would you do to encourage the cooperation of my fourteen-year-old who deliberately makes a nuisance of himself? He throws his clothes around, refuses to help out with any routine tasks in the house, and pesters his little brother perpetually.

I would seek to find a way to link his behavior to something important to the fourteen-year-old, such as privileges or even money. If he receives an allowance, for example, this money could provide an excellent tool with which you can generate a little motivation. Suppose he is given two dollars a week. That maximum can be taxed regularly for violation of predetermined rules. For example, each article of clothing left on the floor might cost him a dime. A deliberate provocation of his brother would subtract a quarter from his total. Each Saturday, he would receive the money remaining from the taxation of the last week. This system conforms to the principle behind all adolescent discipline: give the individual reason for obeying other than the simple fact that he was told to do so.[15]

I have a fourteen-year-old daughter, Margretta, who wants to date a seventeen-year-old boy. I don't feel good about letting her go, but I'm not sure just how to respond. What should I say to her?

Rather than stamping your foot and screaming, "No! And that's semi-final!" I would work out a reasonable plan for the years ahead and a rationale to support it. You might say, "Margretta, you are fourteen years old and I understand your new interest in boys. That's the way it's supposed to be. However, you are not ready to handle the pressures that an older boy can put on a girl your age." (Explain what you mean if she asks.)

"Your dad and I want to help you get ready for dating in the future, but there are some in-between steps you need to take. You have to learn how to be 'friends' with boys before you become a 'lover' with one. To do this, you should get acquainted in groups of boys or girls your age. We'll invite them to our house or you can go to the homes of others. Then when you are between fifteen and sixteen, you can begin double-dating to places that are chaperoned by adults. And finally, you can go on single dates sometime during your sixteenth year.

"Your dad and I want you to date and have fun with boys, and we intend to be reasonable about this. But you're not ready to plunge into single dating with a high school senior, and we'll just have to find other ways to satisfy your social needs."[16]

My unmarried daughter recently told me that she is three months pregnant. What should be my attitude toward her now?

You cannot reverse the circumstances by being harsh or unloving at this point. Your daughter needs more understanding now than ever before, and you should give it to her if possible. Help her grope through this difficulty and avoid "I told you so" comments. She will face many important decisions in the next few months and she will need a calm, rational mother and father to assist in determining the best path to take. Remember that lasting love and affection often develop between people who have survived a crisis together.[17]

My fifteen-year-old is a nature-lover through and through. His room is filled with caged snakes, wasp nests, plants, and insects. Even the garage is occupied by various animals he has caught and tamed. I hate all this stinky stuff and want him to get interested in something else. What should I do?

If he keeps his zoo clean and well managed, then you should let him follow his interests. Just remember that at fifteen, "bugs" beat "drugs" as a hobby![18]

Most teenagers know that drug use is harmful to their bodies and can even kill them. Why, then, do they do it? Are they usually the victims of unscrupulous "pushers" who get them hooked on narcotics?

Not usually. The introduction to drug usage is usually made from friend to friend in a social atmosphere. Marijuana and pills are frequently distributed at parties where a nonuser cannot refuse to participate without appearing square and unsophisticated. Many teenagers would literally risk their lives if they thought their peer group demanded them to do so, and this need for social approval is instrumental in the initiation of most drug habits.[19]

What should parents look for as symptoms of drug abuse?

Listed below are eight physical and emotional symptoms that may indicate substance abuse by your child.

1. Inflammation of the eyelids and nose is common. The pupils of the eyes are either very wide or very small, depending on the kind of drugs internalized.

2. Extremes of energy may be represented. Either the individual is sluggish, gloomy, and withdrawn, or he may be loud, hysterical, and jumpy.

3. The appetite is extreme—either very great or very poor. Weight loss may occur.

4. The personality suddenly changes; the individual may become irritable, inattentive, and confused, or aggressive, suspicious, and explosive.

5. Body and breath odor is often bad. Cleanliness is generally ignored.

6. The digestive system may be upset—diarrhea, nausea, and vomiting may occur. Headaches and double vision are also

common. Other signs of physical deterioration may include change in skin tone and body stance.

7. Needle marks on the body, usually appearing on the arms, are an important symptom. These punctures sometimes get infected and appear as sores and boils.

8. Moral values often crumble and are replaced by new, way-out ideas and values.[20]

Do you think better education is the answer to the drug abuse problem among teenagers?

Unfortunately, narcotics usage among teenagers will not be conquered by instructional programs that explain its hazards. The kids already know the consequences of drug use—probably better than their parents do. They are not deaf, and their abuse of substances is usually done *in spite of* the obvious price tag. Though we have to support our educational efforts with the young (it is our only hope for change), the drug problem will continue until it is no longer fashionable to "trip out." When it becomes disgraceful to use drugs, the epidemic will be over—but not a minute sooner.[21]

How can I help my child withstand the adolescent pressure to conform on important matters such as drug use and sexual immorality?

It is important for your preteenager to know about group pressure before it reaches its peak. Someday he may be sitting in a car with four friends who decide to take some little red pills, and he needs to know *in advance* how he will handle that moment. Roleplay that moment with him, teaching him what to say and do. Your preparation is no guarantee that he will have the courage to stand alone at that crucial time, but his knowledge of peer influence could provide the independence to do what is right. I would, therefore, recommend that this matter of conformity be thoroughly discussed and rehearsed with your ten- or eleven-year-old.[22]

You have described adolescent conformity in graphic detail, and we recognize it in our teenage daughter. But what about adults in the Western culture? Are we also vulnerable to group pressure and conformity?

One of the great American myths is that we are a nation of rugged individualists. We really have ourselves fooled at this point. We like to think of ourselves as Abraham Lincolns, Patrick Henrys, and cowboys, standing tall and courageous in the face of social rejection. But that image is palpably uncharacteristic of most Americans. In truth, we are a nation of social cowards. It seems to me that a major proportion of our energy is expended in trying to be like everyone else, cringing in fear of true individuality.

There are numerous exceptions to this generalization, of course, but social independence and confidence do not appear to be predominant characteristics in the American psyche.

How do you feel about the dangers of marijuana usage today? I've heard that it isn't addictive and therefore isn't harmful; I've also heard that it is very dangerous. What are the facts?
Let me permit Harold Voth, M.D., to speak to that question. Dr. Voth has served as senior psychiatrist and psychoanalyst for the Menninger Foundation in Topeka, Kansas, and is also associate chief of psychiatry for education at Topeka Veterans Administration Medical Center, Topeka, Kansas. These are his words:

> My own family has provided a major stimulus for me to become involved in the problem of drug abuse. Seeing our three sons grow into wholesome manhood provides such a vivid contrast to those youngsters I have observed over the years whose lives have been damaged or destroyed by marijuana.
>
> Witnessing a young person harm himself is a tragic sight; it is heartbreaking. I think of what might have been for all of them, of their parents' broken dreams and of the sadness that has beclouded the lives of their families.
>
> Therefore, to prevent others from walking down the path of deception offered the potential drug user, I refer you to the following facts.
>
> • All parties agree, even those dedicated to the legalization and open distribution of marijuana, that children, teenagers, and young adults whose minds and bodies have not yet matured, as well as pregnant women, should never smoke marijuana.

- 90% of those using hard drugs such as heroin started with marijuana.
- Five marijuana cigarettes have the same cancer causing capacity as 112 conventional cigarettes.
- Marijuana stays in the body, lodged in the fat cells, for three to five weeks. Mental and physical performance is negatively affected during this entire period of time.
- A person smoking marijuana on a regular basis suffers from a cumulative build-up and storage of THC, a toxic chemical, in the fat cells of the body, particularly in the brain. It takes three to five months to detoxify effectively a regular user.
- The part of the brain that allows a person to focus, concentrate, create, learn and conceptualize at an advanced level is still growing during the teenage years. Continuous use of marijuana over a period of time will retard the normal growth of these brain cells.
- A study at Columbia University revealed that female marijuana smokers suffer a sharp increase in cells with damaged DNA (the chemical that carries the genetic code). It was also found that the female reproductive eggs are especially vulnerable to damage by marijuana.
- A second Columbia University study found that a control group smoking a single marijuana cigarette every other day for a year, had a white blood cell count that was 39% lower than normal, thus damaging the immune system and making the user far more susceptible to infection and sickness.
- One marijuana cigarette causes a 41% decrease in driving skills. Two cigarettes cause a 63% decrease.

How can I recognize the symptoms of marijuana use in my sixteen-year-old son?
According to Drug Abuse Central in San Antonio, Texas, the symptoms of marijuana use are as follows:

1. Diminished drive, reduced ambition.
2. Significant drop in the quality of school work.
3. Reduced attention span.
4. Impaired communication skills.
5. Distinct lessening in social warmth; less care for the feelings of others.

6. Pale face, imprecise eye movements, red eyes.
7. Neglect of personal appearance.
8. Inappropriate overreaction to mild criticism.
9. A change from active competitive interests to a more passive, withdrawn personality.
10. Association with friends who refuse to identify themselves or simply hang up if parents answer the phone.
11. An increased secretiveness about money or the disappearance of money or valuables from the house.

You've expressed strong opinions about the need for mothers to be at home when their children are small. How do you feel about the mothers of elementary and high school students being employed outside the home?

If you had asked me this question five years ago, I would have said that mothers are needed at home primarily during the preschool years. After kindergarten, the critical factor is to be there when the kids get home from school. That would have been my reply when our children were five years younger. But now that Danae is sixteen and Ryan is eleven, I feel even more strongly about the need for mothers to be at home during the adolescent years. This will not be a popular view, but I can only report honestly what I feel and have observed.

The frantic activities of teenagers create great stresses on families which require adult attention. Who will be there to taxi the kids back and forth and get ready for the slumber party and sew the new dress and attend the first football game and keep up with all the "must dos" of those years? Not only is Mom needed to hold things together at home during these pressurized days, but she must brace herself for the conflict so typical of these years. It is not a good time for her to come home exhausted each evening from a job that has required her total commitment. That sets the stage for emotional explosions between generations.

SECTION 14

QUESTIONS FROM ADOLESCENTS

I am a teenager and I want to look and dress just like all my friends. My parents tell me I should be an individual and be willing to be different, but I just can't do it. Do *you* understand?

Sure I do. Let me explain why you feel such pressure to be like everyone else. The answer involves feelings of inferiority, which are usually very strong during adolescence. You see, when you feel worthless and foolish—when you don't like yourself—then you are more frightened by the threat of ridicule or rejection by your friends. You become more sensitive about being laughed at. You lack the confidence to be different. Your problems seem bad enough without making them worse by defying the wishes of the majority. So you dress the way they tell you to dress, and you talk the way they tell you to talk, and all your ideas are the group's ideas. You become afraid to raise your hand in class or express your own ideas. Your great desire is to behave in the "safest" way possible. These behaviors all have one thing in common: they result from a lack of self-confidence.

Gradually, your self-respect will return as you become more mature and comfortable with the person God made you to be.[1]

I am fourteen and I have crummy-looking pimples all over my face. What causes them and what can I do to clear up my skin?

Practically every part of your body is affected in one way or another by the period of change you are now experiencing. Even your skin undergoes major changes, whether you are a boy or a girl. In fact, this is probably the most distressing aspect of all the physical events that take place in early adolescence. A study of two thousand teenagers asked the question, "What do you most dislike about yourself?" Skin problems outranked every other reply by a wide margin.

Skin eruptions occur primarily as a result of an oily substance which is secreted during adolescence. The pores of the skin tend to fill up with this oil and become blocked. Since the oil can't escape, it hardens there and causes pimples or blackheads. You might expect to have these imperfections on your skin for several years, although some cases are milder than others.

When you get numerous pimples and blackheads regularly, the condition is called acne. If this happens, it will be very important for you to keep your skin clean, minimizing the oil and dirt on your face. We used to think that certain greasy foods and chocolate contributed to the difficulty, but doctors now doubt this relationship. If the problem is severe, as you obviously feel it is, you should ask your parents to take you to a dermatologist, who is a doctor specializing in skin problems. Acne can now be treated effectively in most cases.[2]

I am thirteen and I feel miserable about myself. Is there anything I can do?

First, you need to understand that you are not alone. Begin observing the people around you and see if you detect hidden feelings of inferiority. When you go to school tomorrow, quietly watch the students who are coming and going. I assure you, many of them have the same concerns that trouble you. They reveal these doubts by being very shy and quiet, by being extremely angry and mean, by being silly, by being afraid to participate in a game or a contest, by blushing frequently, or by acting proud and "stuck-up." You'll soon learn to recognize the signs of inferiority, and then you'll know that it is a *very* common disorder! Once you fully comprehend that others feel as you do, then you *should never again* feel alone. It will give you more confidence to know that everyone is afraid of embarrassment and ridicule—that we're all sitting in the same leaky boat, trying to plug the watery holes. And would you believe, I nearly drowned in that same leaky boat when I was fourteen years old?

Second, I advise you to look squarely at the worries that keep gnawing at you from the back of your mind or from deep within your heart, causing a black cloud to hang over your head day and night. It would be a good idea to get alone, where there is no one to interfere with your thoughts. Then *list* all the things which you most dislike about yourself. Nobody is going to see this paper except the people to whom you choose to show it, so you can be completely honest. Write down everything that has been bothering you. Even admit the characteristics that you dislike, including the tendency to get mad and blow up (if that applies to you).

Identify your most serious problems as best as possible. Do you get frustrated and angry at people and then feel bad later? Or is it your shyness that makes you afraid when you're with other people? Is it your inability to express your ideas—to put your thoughts into words? Is it your laziness, your unkindness to other people, or the way you look? Whatever concerns you, write it down as best you can. Then when you're finished, go back through the list and put a mark by those items that worry you the most— the problems that you spend the most time thinking and fretting about.

Third, think about each item on the list. Give your greatest creative thought to what might be done to change the things you don't like. If you wish, you might share the paper with your pastor, counselor, parent, or someone in whom you have confidence: that person can then help you map out a plan for improvement. You'll feel better for having faced your problems, and you might even find genuine solutions to some of the troublesome matters.

Now, we come to an important step. The key to mental health is being able to accept what you cannot change. After you've done what you can to deal with your problems, I feel you should take the paper on which the most painful items are written, and burn it in a private ceremony before God. Commit your life to Him once more—strengths and weaknesses—good points and bad—asking Him to take what you have and bless it. After all, He created the entire universe from nothing, and He can make something beautiful out of your life.[3]

I am also a teenager, and I have a very hard time making friends. Can you help me learn how to influence people and make them like me?

"The best way to *have* a friend is to *be* a good friend to others." That's a very old proverb, but it's still true. Now let me give you a little clue that will help you deal with people of *any* age. Most people experience feelings of inferiority and self-doubt, as I have described. And if you understand and remember that fact, it will help you know the secret of social success. *Never* make fun of others or ridicule them. Let them know that you respect and accept them, and that they are important to you. Make a conscious effort to be sensitive to their feelings, and protect their reputations. I think you'll quickly find that many will do the same for you in return.[4]

I'm twelve years old and my dad tells me my body will soon change a lot. It's already happened to some of the other guys I know. But I don't understand what's about to happen to me or why. Would you sort of fill me in?
I'd be glad to. The growing up process is a wonderful and interesting event. It's all controlled by a tiny organ near the center of your brain called the *pituitary gland.* This little organ is only the size of a small bean, yet it's called the master gland because it tells the rest of your glands what to do. It's the "big boss upstairs," and when it screams, your glandular system jumps. Somewhere within your own pituitary gland is a plan for your body. At just the right time, it will send out chemical messengers, called hormones, which will tell the rest of the glands in your body, "Get moving, it's time to grow up." In fact, those hormones will have many implications for your body during the next few years of your life.

I'm glad your dad told you about the changes soon to occur. There are several reasons why you ought to understand this aspect of physical development. First, if you don't know what is about to happen to your body, it can be pretty terrifying when everything goes crazy all at one time. It's not unusual for a teenager to begin worrying about himself. He wonders, "What's going on here? Do I have a disease? Could this be cancer? Is there something wrong with my body? Dare I discuss it with anybody?" These are unnecessary fears that result from ignorance or misinformation about the body. When young people understand the process, they know that these changes represent normal, natural events which they should have been anticipating. So I'm going to tell you exactly what you can expect in the period of early adolescence. There's just no reason for you to be anxious over these rapid physical changes.

The most important change that you will notice is that your body will begin to prepare itself for parenthood. Now I didn't say that you are about to become a parent (that should be years away), but that your body is about to *equip itself* with the ability to produce a child. That's one of the major changes that occurs during this period. The correct name for this time of sexual awakening is *puberty.*

During puberty, you will begin to grow very rapidly, faster than ever before in your life. Your muscles will become much more like those of a man, and you'll get much stronger and better coordinated. That's why a junior high boy is usually a much better athlete than a fifth or sixth grader, and why a high school boy is a better athlete than a junior high boy. A dramatic increase occurs in his overall body size, strength, and coordination during this period.

Second, your hair will begin to look more like the hair of a man. You'll notice the beginnings of a beard on your face, and you'll have to start shaving it every now and then. Hair will also grow under your arms for the first time, and also on what is called the pubic region (or what you may have called the private area), around your sex organs. The sex organs themselves will become larger and more like those of an adult male. These are evidences that the little boy is disappearing forever, and in his place will come a man, capable of becoming a father and taking care of his wife and family. This fantastic transformation reminds me in some ways of a caterpillar, which spins a cocoon around itself and then after awhile comes out as a totally different creature—a butterfly. Of course the changes in a boy are not that complete, but you will never be the same after undergoing this process of *maturation* (the medical word for growing up).

These rapid changes are probably just around the corner for you. The frightening thing for some kids is that they occur very suddenly, almost overnight. The pituitary gland quickly begins kicking everything into action. It barks its orders right and left, and your entire body seems to race around inside, trying to carry out these commands.

Everything is affected—even your voice will be different. I'm sure you've noticed how much lower your dad's voice is than your own. Have you ever wondered how it got that way? Was it always deep and gruff? Did it always sound like a foghorn? Can you imagine your dad in his crib as a baby saying "Goo, goo" in a deep voice? Of course not. He wasn't born that way. His voice changed during puberty, and that's what will happen to yours, too. However an adolescent boy's voice is sometimes an embarrassment to him until this deepening process is finished, because it doesn't sound very solid. It squeaks and screeches and wobbles and cracks for a few months. But again, this is nothing to worry about, because the voice will soon be deep and steady. A little time is needed to complete this development of the vocal cords.

Another physical problem occurring with both boys and girls during puberty is fatigue, or lack of energy. Your body will be investing so many of its resources into the growing process that it will seem to lack energy for other activities for a period of time. This phase usually doesn't last very long. However, this tired feeling is something you ought to anticipate. In fact, it should influence your behavior in two ways.

First, you must get plenty of sleep and rest during the period of rapid growth. That need is often not met, however, because teenagers feel that they should not have to go to bed as early as they did when they were children. Therefore, they stay up too late and then drag through the next day in a state of exhaustion. Believe it or not, a twelve- or thirteen-year-old person actually needs more rest than when he was nine or ten, simply because of the acceleration in growth.

Second, the foods you eat will also be very important during adolescence. Your body has to have the raw materials with which to construct those new muscle cells and bones and fibers that are in the plans. It will be necessary for you to get a *balanced* diet during this time; it's even more important than when you were six or eight. If you don't eat right during this growth period, you will pay the price with sickness and various physical problems. Your body *must* have the vitamins and minerals and protein necessary to enlarge itself in so many ways.

These are some of the basic changes you can expect within a few years. And when they have occurred, you will be on your way to manhood.[5]

My name is Kim. I am eleven and am a girl. What changes can I expect to take place? I'm especially interested in menstruation and how babies are made.
A girl's body goes through even more complex changes than those of a boy, because it has to prepare itself for the very complicated task of motherhood. The way a woman's body functions to produce human life is one of the most beautiful mechanisms in all of God's universe. Let's look at that process for a moment.

All human life begins as one tiny cell, so small that you

couldn't see it without a microscope. This first cell of life is called a zygote, which begins to divide and grow inside the mother's uterus.

The uterus is a special place inside the mother's lower abdomen, or what you may have called the stomach. Actually, it's not in the stomach at all, but below it. The uterus is a special little pouch that serves as a perfect environment for a growing and developing embryo. (An *embryo* is the name for a baby in its earliest stages of development.)

All the baby's needs for warmth and oxygen and nourishment are met constantly by the mother's body during the nine months before his birth. Any little slip-up during those very early days (the first three months especially), and the growing child will die. The embryo is extremely delicate, and the mother's body has to be in good physical condition in order to meet the requirements of the growing child.

In order to meet these requirements, a girl's body undergoes many changes during puberty. One of those important developments is called menstruation, which I'm glad you asked about. This is a subject that girls will need to understand thoroughly in the days ahead. Most schools provide this information to girls in the fifth or sixth grade, so what I'll tell you now may just be a review of what you have seen and heard elsewhere. However, I feel it is important for boys to understand this process, too, although they are seldom informed properly.

When a woman becomes pregnant—that is, when the one-celled zygote is planted in her uterus after having a sexual relationship with a man—her body begins to protect this embryo and help it grow. It has to have oxygen and food and many chemicals which are necessary for life. The substances are delivered to the uterus automatically, through the mother's blood. But since the uterus has no way of knowing when a new life is going to be planted there, it must get ready to receive an embryo each month, just in case it happens. Therefore, blood accumulates on the walls of the uterus in order to nourish an embryo if the woman becomes pregnant. But if she *doesn't* become pregnant that month, then the uterine blood is not needed. It is released from the walls of the uterus and flows out through the vagina—that special opening through which babies are also born.

Every twenty-eight days (this number varies a bit from person to person), a woman's body will get rid of this unnecessary blood which would have been used to nourish a baby if she had become pregnant. It usually takes about three to five days for the flow to stop, and during this time she wears a kind of cloth pad to absorb the blood. This process is called *menstruation*.

There are some very important attitudes that I want you to understand through this discussion. First, menstruation is not something for girls to dread and fear. Since the subject of blood causes us to shudder, some girls get very tense over this process happening to them. They start worrying about it and dreading its arrival, and some do not want it to happen at all. But actually, menstruation makes possible the most fantastic and exciting event that can ever occur— the creation of a new human being. What a miracle it is for a single cell, the zygote, to quietly split into two, then four, eight, and sixteen cells, and continue to divide until trillions of new cells are formed! A little heart slowly emerges within the cluster of cells, and begins beating to the rhythm of life. Then come fingers and toes and eyes and ears and all the internal organs. A special liquid (called amniotic fluid) surrounds the baby to protect him from any bumps or bruises the mother might receive. And there he stays for nine months, until he is capable of surviving in the world outside. Then at just the right moment the mother's body begins pushing the baby down the birth canal (the vagina) and into the waiting hands of the physician.

The most beautiful aspect of this incredibly complicated system is that it all works *automatically* within a woman's body. It's almost as though the Master Designer, God Himself, were standing nearby, telling her what to do next. In fact, did you know that this is precisely what happens? We are told by King David, writing in the Psalms, that God is present during this creation of a new life. Let's read his description of that event:

> You made all the delicate, inner parts of my body, and knit them together in my mother's womb. Thank you for making me so wonderfully complex! It is amazing to think about. Your workmanship is marvelous—and how well I know it. You were there while I was being formed in utter seclusion! (Psa. 139:13-15 TLB).

Not only did God supervise David's development in his mother's womb (another word for uterus), but He did the same thing for you and me! He has also scheduled each day of our lives and recorded every day in His book. That is the most reassuring thought that I've ever known!

So you see, menstruation is not an awful event for girls to dread. It is a signal that the body is preparing itself to cooperate with God in creating a new life, if that proves to be His will for a particular woman. Menstruation is the body's way of telling a girl that she is growing up . . . that she is not a child anymore . . . and that something very exciting is happening inside.

Now, Kim, please don't worry about this aspect of your health. You will not bleed to death, I promise you. Menstruation is as natural as eating or sleeping or any other bodily process. If you feel you are abnormal in some way—if you're worried about some aspect of menstruation—if you think you're different or that maybe something has gone wrong—or if there's some pain associated with your menstruation or you have any question at all, then muster your courage and talk to your mother or your doctor or someone in whom you have confidence. In about 98 cases out of 100, the fears will prove to be unjustified. You will find that you are completely normal, and that the trouble was only in your lack of understanding of the mechanism.

Now, obviously, other things will begin to happen to your body at about the same time as menstruation. You will probably have a growth spurt just prior to your first menstruation. (Incidentally, the average age of first menstruation in American girls is now about twelve-and-a-half years of age, but it can occur as early as nine or ten years or as late as sixteen or seventeen. The age varies widely from girl to girl.)

During this time your body will become more rounded and curvy like your mother's. Your breasts will enlarge, and they may become sore occasionally (boys sometimes experience this soreness, too). This doesn't mean that you have cancer or some other disease, but simply that your breasts are changing, like everything else in your body. Hair will also grow under your arms, on your legs, and in the pubic region, as with boys. These are the most obvious physical changes which take place, and when you see them happening you can kiss good-bye to childhood—it's full speed ahead toward adulthood.[6]

I am thirteen-and-a-half and I haven't started to change yet. I'm shorter and not as strong as most of my friends. And they have voices that are lower than mine. It's

embarrassing! I don't even have hair down below yet! Is there anything wrong with me?

No. There is nothing wrong with you. You are just progressing on your own timetable. It's just as healthy to grow up later as earlier, and there's no reason to fear that you will never mature. Just hold steady for a year or two, and then the fireworks will all begin to pop for you, just as for everybody else! I can promise you that this is going to happen. If you don't believe me, take a look at all the adults around you. Do you see any of them that look like children? Of course not. *Everyone* grows up sooner or later.

Certainly it's never much fun to be laughed at by your friends, but if you know you'll be different for only a short time, maybe you can stand it. Most importantly, don't you be guilty of making another person feel bad about himself if you happen to grow before he does![7]

Can I ask you a question about sex? I want to know more about making babies and all that stuff that my older brother talks about.

That's a very important question and I'm glad you asked it. As your body starts to change, you'll notice that you're beginning to be more interested in people of the opposite sex. Suddenly girls begin to look great to boys and the boys start appealing to the girls. How do I know this will happen? How can I predict it so accurately? Because sex will soon become an "appetite" within you. If you missed your breakfast this morning, I can predict that you'll be plenty hungry by two o'clock in the afternoon. Your body will ask for food. It's made that way. There are chemicals in your body that will make you feel hungry when you haven't eaten.

In the same way, some new chemicals in your body will begin to develop a brand-new appetite when you're between twelve and fifteen years old. This will not be a craving for food, but it will involve the matter called sex, or the male or female aspects of your nature. Every year as you get older, this appetite will become more and more a part of you. You'll want to spend more of your time with someone of the opposite sex. Eventually this desire may lead you to marriage. Marriage is a wonderful union for those who find the right person. However, let me offer a word of caution on that subject.

One of the biggest mistakes you can make with your life is to get married *too soon*. That can be tragic. I want to stress that point in your mind. For two people to get married before they are ready can be a disaster. Unfortunately, this happens all too frequently. I will say more about this subject later in the book, but I strongly advise you not to get married until you're at least twenty years of age. *Half of all teenage marriages* blow up within five years, causing many tears and problems. I don't want yours to be one of those broken homes.

Now let me describe for you the feeling that sex will bring in the next few years. Boys will become very interested in the bodies of girls—in the way they're built, in their curves and soft-ness, and in their pretty hair and eyes. Even their feminine feet may have an appeal to boys during this time. If you're a boy, it's very likely that you will think often about these fascinating creatures called girls, whom you used to hate so much! In fact, the sexual appetite is stronger in males between sixteen and eighteen years of age than at any other age in life.

Girls, on the other hand, will not be quite so excited over the shape and the look of a boy's body (although they will find them interesting). They will be more fascinated by the boy himself— the way he talks, the way he walks, the way he thinks. If you're a girl, you will probably get a "crush" on one boy after another. (A crush occurs when you begin to think that one particular per-son is absolutely fantastic, and you fantasize about the possibility of being married to that person. It is not uncommon to get a crush on a teacher or a pastor or older man. Usually crushes are constantly changing, lasting only a few weeks or months before another one takes its place.)

Now we need to talk very plainly about the subject of sexual intercourse, which is the name given to the act that takes place when a man and a woman remove all their clothing (usually done in bed) and the man's sex organ (his *penis*) becomes very hard and straight. He puts his penis into the vagina of the woman while lying between her legs. They move around, in and out, until they both have a kind of tingly feeling which lasts for a minute or two. It's a very satisfying experience, which hus-bands and wives do regularly. You probably already know about sexual intercourse as I described it. But did you know that a man and woman do not have intercourse just to have babies? They do it to express love for each other and because they enjoy doing it. In this way they satisfy each other. They may have sex-ual intercourse two or three times a week, or maybe only once a month; each couple is different. But this is a fun part of marriage, and something that makes a husband and wife very special to each other. This is an act which they save just for each other.

This appetite for sex is something that God created within you. I want to make this point very strongly. Sex is not dirty and it is not evil. Nothing that God ever created could be dirty. The desire for sex was God's idea—not ours. He placed this part of our nature in us; He created those chemicals (hormones) that make the opposite sex appealing to us. He did this so we would want to have a family of our own. Without this desire there would be no marriage and no children and no love between a man and a woman. So sex is not a dirty thing at all; it's a wonderful, beautiful mechanism, no matter what you may have heard about it.

However, I must also tell you that God intends for us to control that desire for sexual intercourse. He has stated repeatedly in the Bible that we are to save our body for the person we will eventually marry, and that it is wrong to satisfy our appetite for sex with a boy or girl before we get married. There is just no other way to interpret the biblical message. Some of your friends may tell you differently in the days ahead. You may hear Jack or Susie or Paul or Jane tell about how they explored each other's bodies. They'll tell you how exciting it was, and try to get you to do the same.

Let me state it more personally. It is very likely that *you* will have a chance to have sexual intercourse before you reach twenty years of age. Sooner or later that opportunity will come to you. You will be with a person of the opposite sex who will let you know that he or she will permit you to have this experience. You're going to have to decide between now and then what you'll do about that moment when it comes. You probably won't have time to think when it suddenly happens. My strongest advice is for you to decide *right now* to save your body for the one who will eventually be your marriage partner. If you don't control this desire you will later wish that you had.

God's commandment that we avoid sexual intercourse before marriage was not given in order to keep us from having pleasure. It was not His desire to take the fun out of life. To the contrary, it was actually His *love* that caused Him to forbid premarital intercourse, because so many harmful consequences occur when you refuse to obey Him.

You've probably heard about venereal disease, which is

caused from having intercourse with someone who has caught it from another carrier. Syphilis, gonorrhea, and other diseases are very widespread today. Our country is having an epidemic of these diseases, and they have a damaging effect on the body if they go untreated. But there are other consequences for those who have premarital sex. They run the risk of bringing an unwanted baby into the world by this act. When that occurs, they face the responsibility of raising a human being—a little life with all its needs for love and discipline and the stability of a home—but they have no way to take care of him or meet his needs. That is tragic.

But just as serious are the changes that take place within a person's *mind* when he has intercourse outside the bonds of marriage. First, and most important, his relationship with God is sacrificed. Premarital sex is a sin, and a person can't be friends with God if he is going to continue to sin deliberately and willfully. First John 1:6 says, "If we say we are his friends but go on living in spiritual darkness and sin, we are lying" (TLB). It's as simple as that. Furthermore, nothing can be hidden from God, as you know, because He sees everything.

Sin always has a destructive effect on a young person. But I believe the sin of premarital sex is especially damaging to the young person who engages in it. He or she loses the innocence of youth, and sometimes becomes hard and cold as a person. It's also likely to affect his or her later marriage, because that special experience which should have been shared with just one person is not so special anymore. More than one person has had a sample of it.

So you see, there are many obvious reasons why God has told us to control our sexual desires. What I'm saying is that God has commanded us not to have sex before marriage in order to spare us these many other effects of this sin. In fact, the *worst* consequence is one I have not yet mentioned, relating to the judgment of God in the life to come. We are told very clearly in the Bible that our lives will be laid bare before Him, and He will know every secret. Our eternal destinies actually depend on our faith in God and our obedience to Him.

I hope this has answered your question. There is so much more I could say if time permitted. Why don't you make a list of additional questions to discuss with your father or youth leader at church?[8]

What are wet dreams that I hear other boys talking about?

Many boys have "wet dreams," or what doctors call *nocturnal emissions*. This refers to the fluid which comes out of a boy's penis occasionally at night. The fluid is called semen, and contains millions of cells so tiny that you can't even see them. One of these cells could become a child if it were injected into a female and combined with her egg cell. (That would compose the zygote which we discussed earlier.) This semen sometimes is released during a nighttime dream; then the boy finds the stain on his pajamas the next morning and begins to worry about what is going on. However, this event is perfectly normal. It happens to almost all boys, and is nothing to worry about. A nocturnal emission is just his body's way of getting rid of the extra fluid that has accumulated.[9]

Is there anything else I need to know about growing up that I haven't thought to ask?

Just that many young people worry about their bodies unnecessarily during this time. These kinds of questions plague them:

1. Are all these changes supposed to be happening?
2. Is there something wrong with me?
3. Do I have a disease or an abnormality?
4. Am I going to be different from other people?
5. Does this pain in my breast mean I have cancer? (Remember, I mentioned that the breasts sometimes get sore during adolescence.)
6. Will I be able to have intercourse, or will there be something wrong with me?
7. Will the boys laugh at me? Will the girls reject me? (It's very common for people to feel they're not going to be attractive to the opposite sex and that nobody will want them because they are not as pretty or handsome as they wish they could be.)
8. Will God punish me for the sexual thoughts that I have? (I told you that you're likely to think about the opposite sex often during these years. When this happens you may feel guilty for the thoughts that occur.)
9. Wouldn't it be awful if I became a homosexual? (A homosexual is someone who is not attracted to the opposite sex, but who is attracted to the *same* sex. It's a boy's interest in boys or a girl's interest in girls. Homosexuality is an abnormal desire that

reflects deep problems, but it doesn't happen very often and it's not likely to happen to you.)

10. Could I get pregnant without having sexual relations? (This is another possibility that some young girls fear—that they could find themselves pregnant even if they haven't had sexual relations. I want you to know that this *never* happens; it's an impossibility. Only one time in all of history did this occur, and that's when the Virgin Mary, Jesus' mother, became pregnant even though she had never had sexual intercourse. Jesus was conceived or planted in her uterus by God Himself. That's the only time in the world's history that a human being has ever been born without the father doing his part by providing half of the cell that becomes the zygote.)

11. Do some people fail to mature sexually? (Any system of the body can malfunction, but this one *rarely* fails.)

12. Will my modesty be sacrificed? (It's common during the early adolescent years for you to become extremely modest about your body. You know it's changing and you don't want anybody to see it. Therefore, you may worry about being in a doctor's office and having to take off your clothes in front of other people.)

Let me say it one more time: these kinds of fears are almost universal during the early years of adolescence. Nearly everyone growing up in our culture worries and frets over the subject of sex. I want to help you avoid those anxieties. Your sexual development is a normal event that is being controlled inside your body. It will work out all right, so you can just relax and let it happen. However, you will have to control your sexual desires in the years ahead, and that will require determination and willpower. But if you can learn to channel your sexual impulses the way God intended, this part of your nature can be one of the most fascinating and wonderful aspects of your life, perhaps contributing to a successful and happy marriage in the years ahead.[10]

TELEVISION AND VIOLENCE

**What is your view of TV, generally? Should parents
attempt to regulate what their children watch?**
Most television programming is awful! According to Dr. Gerald
Looney, University of Arizona, by the time the average
preschool child reaches fourteen years of age, he will have
witnessed 18,000 murders on TV, and countless hours of related
violence, nonsense, and unadulterated drivel! Dr. Saul Kapel
states, furthermore, that the most time-consuming activity in
the life of a child is neither school nor family interaction. It is
television, absorbing 14,000 valuable hours during the course
of childhood! That is equivalent to sitting before the tube eight
hours a day, continuously for 4.9 years!

There are other aspects of television which demand its
regulation and controls. For one thing, it is an enemy of
communication within the family. How can we talk to each
other when a million-dollar production in living color is always
beckoning our attention? I am also concerned about the current
fashion whereby each program director is compelled to include
all the avant-garde ideas—go a little farther—use a little more
profanity—discuss the undiscussable—assault the public
concept of good taste and decency. In so doing, they are hacking
away at the foundations of the family and all that represents the
Christian ethic. In recent seasons, for example, we were offered
hilariously funny episodes involving abortion, divorce,
extramarital relationships, rape, and the ever-popular theme,
"Father is an idiot." If this is "social relevance," then I am sick
unto death of the messages I have been fed.

Television, with its unparalleled capacity for teaching and
edifying, has occasionally demonstrated the potential it carries.

"Little House on the Prairie" was for years the best program available for young children. I would not, therefore, recommend smashing the television set in despair. Rather, we must learn to control it instead of becoming its slave. When our children were young, they were permitted to watch one hour of cartoons on Saturday morning and a one-half hour program each afternoon, selected from an approved list. That still sounds like a reasonable schedule for elementary school children.[1]

Since there are so many problems about the use of television in the home, wouldn't it be better just to get rid of our TV set until after our children are grown up?
Some families have done just that, and I admire their courage in doing so. But I think it is *possible* to keep our television sets without being dominated by them. I would suggest that the entire family get together to talk specifically about television—what's wrong with it, how it can be managed, and how children can learn to be discerning and selective in their use of the TV set.

Furthermore, it is important for parents to watch television *with* their children, not only helping them understand what they are experiencing, but as a pleasant family activity. Watching TV together can be a wonderful springboard into various kinds of teaching and discussion if it is approached properly.

I am also concerned about the impact of television in our home. How can we control it without resorting to dictatorial rules and regulations?
It seems that we have three objectives as parents. First, we want to monitor the *quality* of the programs our children watch. Second, we want to regulate the *quantity* of television they see. Even good programs may have an undesirable influence on the rest of children's activities if they spend too much time in front of the tube. Third, we should include the entire family in establishing a TV policy, if possible.

I read about a system recently that is very effective in accomplishing all three of these purposes. First, it was suggested that parents sit down with the children and select a list of approved programs that are appropriate for each age level. Then type that list (or at least write it clearly) and enclose it in clear plastic so it can be referred to throughout the week.

Second, either buy or make a roll of tickets. Issue each child ten tickets per week, and let him use them to "buy" the privilege of watching the programs on the approved list. When his tickets are gone, then his television viewing is over for that week. This teaches him to choose carefully what he most wants to spend his time on. Ten hours a week is perhaps a good target to shoot at. I'm told that the average preschool child watches up to fifty-four hours of television per week. That's far too much, even for an elementary child.

This system can be modified to fit individual home situations or circumstances. If there's a special program that all the children want to see, such as a Charlie Brown feature or a holiday program during Christmas and Thanksgiving, you can issue more tickets. You might also give extra tickets as rewards for achievement or some other laudable behavior.

The real test will occur when parents reveal whether or not they have the courage to put themselves on that same limited system, too. We often need the same regulations in our viewing habits![2]

What can we do about the violence and decadence of television?

We have a lot more power to influence television than we think we do. I'm told that every letter that producers receive is estimated to represent 40,000 viewers who feel the same way but did not take time to sit down and write. But it's important to know whom we should write. I have sometimes written directors and producers and executives of television networks, and haven't felt that it made much difference. I've found it's more beneficial to write the sponsors—the people who are paying the bills. They are very responsive to our viewpoint because the reason they are supporting the program is to try to win our allegiance for their products. We can bring pressure to bear upon them by letting them know that we do not agree with what's going on. And indeed, we must![3]

There must be a significant psychological factor in the Western culture that lends itself to violence, in addition to the influences of television and literature, etc. How do

you explain our predisposition to killing and acts of violence?

You've asked a perceptive question. In addition to the influence of the entertainment industry, there is another factor which accounts for some of the violence around us. I'm referring to the hostility with which people commonly react to feelings of inferiority today. Everyone who perceives themselves to be short-changed or disrespected by society is expected to be angry, whether they be members of the women's liberation movement, or the gay liberation movement, or the Chicano movement (Brown Berets), or the Jewish Defense League, or the Black civil rights movement, or the handicapped. (Is there anyone left who doesn't belong to *some* oppressed minority?) Feelings of inferiority even account for the outbreak of wars and international hatred. What did Hitler tell the German people in 1939? He assured them that their loss in World War I was the fault of their incompetent leaders; they were really superior human beings. He was capitalizing on their self-doubt as a defeated, humiliated people. I suspect that their willingness to fight was more motivated by this new pride than any other factor. More recently, the 1973 Arab attack on Israel was primarily intended to avenge their disgraceful loss in the Six-Day War of 1967. The world scoffed at the Arab impotence, which was more intolerable than the loss of the land or the death and destruction they sustained. One Arab journalist was quoted in *Time* magazine (October 22, 1973) shortly after the 1973 war began: "It doesn't matter if the Israelis eventually counterattack and drive us back. What matters is that the world now no longer will laugh at us."

Recent evidence even suggests that inferiority is the major force behind the rampaging incidence of rape today. If sexual intercourse were the only objective of a rapist, then he could find satisfaction with a prostitute. But something else is involved. Most rapists apparently want to humiliate their victims. Having been unsuccessful with girls through adolescence and young adulthood, they seek sexual superiority by disgracing and exploiting defenseless women.

How about aggressive violence in American classrooms, which has been increasing steadily in recent years? Can it be attributed to the frustration of low self-esteem? I'm inclined to believe so. And what better explanation can there be for the vandalism which destroys millions of dollars worth of school property each year? Students feel foolish and disrespectful during the day and set about retaliating under the cover of night.

The examples are legion. That is why I have contended that social chaos in all its forms is increased when citizens feel inadequate and inferior. There are numerous other causes, of course, but none so powerful.[4]

Would you comment on the violence in our society at large, and the forces which are propelling it? What do you think can and should be done about it?

There are few subjects that cause me greater concern than the exposure being given to crime and violence in America today. Recently, a squadron of Los Angeles police cornered a desperate gunman in a residential area of the community. The fugitive had barricaded himself in a small house, and held three juvenile hostages inside. Television crews were on hand to photograph one of the children, a teenaged boy, as he was forced outside and then shot in the head by his abductor, who subsequently committed suicide. The pathetic young victim died on the sidewalk in a pool of his own blood. I sat stunned, literally sick to my stomach, while the drama was broadcast in full color last night.

A flood of emotions ran through my mind as I gazed into the immobile, unfocused eyes of the dying adolescent. Mixed with deep pity and remorse was a sudden outpouring of indignation—a revulsion which has been accumulating for years. I was angry at the profiteers who have nurtured violence in our society, and at those millions who seem to thrive on it; I was angry at movie producers like Sam Peckinpah, who have smeared blood and guts all over the silver screen; I was angry at theater patrons for demanding a dozen disembowelments per hour in their visual entertainment; I was angry at television networks for giving us continuous police stories, with their guns and silly automobile chases and karate chops and SWAT teams. I was angry at the Supreme Court for legalizing 1.5 million abortions by American women last year; I was angry at the Palestine Liberation Army for killing eight innocent athletes at the Olympic Games in Munich; I was angry at Truman Capote for writing *In Cold Blood*, and at his thrill-seeking readers for wanting to know how a peaceful family was mercilessly butchered on their farm; and I was particularly angry at the pathetic system of American justice which makes crime so profitable and punishment so improbable.

But my indignation will change nothing and the wave of violence and lawlessness will continue unabated. We have become so desensitized to human suffering and exploitation that even the most horrible events are accepted as part of our regular evening "entertainment" on the tube.

I think it is time that millions of decent, law-abiding citizens rise up with one voice to oppose the industries that are profiting from violence. A valiant campaign of this nature was waged in 1977 by the National Parent Teacher Association, directing their efforts at television networks and companies that support the most damaging programs. Of course, this pressure from the PTA brought an anguished cry of "foul play" from the greedy profiteers whose pockets were lined with blood-stained money. Nevertheless, Sears Roebuck, Union Oil, and other large companies pledged to sponsor no more violent programs on television. This form of economic sanction, more recently headed by Donald Wildmon and the National Federation for Decency, is the most powerful tool available to influence our free enterprise system, and we should use it incisively against those who would destroy us from within. We have sat on our hands long enough![5]

FINAL COMMENT

My purpose in preparing this book has been to verbalize the Judeo-Christian tradition and philosophy regarding family living in its many manifestations. And what is that philosophical foundation? It involves parental control of young children with love and care, a reasonable introduction to self-discipline and responsibility, parental *leadership* which seeks the best interest of the child, respect for the dignity and worth of every member of the family, conformity with the moral laws of God, and it attempts to maximize the physical and mental potential of each individual from infancy forward. That is our game plan. That is the common thread which links the issues and concerns discussed throughout the pages of this book.

If the objectives cited above could be boiled at extreme temperatures until only the essential ingredients remained, these four irreducible values would survive unscathed:

1. A belief in the unestimable worth and significance of human life in all dimensions, including the unborn, the aged, the widowed, the mentally retarded, the unattractive, the physically handicapped, and every other condition in which humanness is expressed from conception to the grave.

2. An unyielding dedication to the institution of marriage as a permanent, life-long relationship, regardless of trials, sickness, financial reverses or emotional stresses that may ensue.

3. A dedication to the task of bearing and raising children, even in a topsy-turvy world that denigrates this procreative privilege.

4. A commitment to the ultimate purpose in living: the attainment of eternal life through Jesus Christ our Lord, beginning within our own families and then reaching out to a suffering humanity that does not know of His love and sacrifice. Compared to this overriding objective, no other human endeavor is of any significance or meaning whatsoever.

The four corners of this Christian perspective have been under severe assault in recent years, yet the philosophy will remain viable for as long as mothers and fathers and children cohabit the face of the earth. It will certainly outlive humanism and the puny efforts of mankind to find an alternative.

NOTES

Key for book abbreviations:

DD — *Dare to Discipline*, Tyndale House Publishers, Wheaton, IL, 1970, trade paper.
EM — *Emotions: Can You Trust Them?* Regal Books, Ventura, CA, 1980.
HS — *Hide or Seek: Self-Esteem for the Child*, Fleming H. Revell Company, Old Tappan, NJ, 1979.
PA — *Preparing for Adolescence*, Vision House Publishers, Santa Ana, CA, 1978.
STTM — *Straight Talk to Men and Their Wives*, Word Books, Waco, TX, 1980.
SWC — *The Strong-Willed Child*, Tyndale House Publishers, Wheaton, IL, 1978.
WWW— *What Wives Wish Their Husbands Knew about Women*, Tyndale House Publishers, Wheaton, IL, 1975.

FF — *Focus on the Family* cassette tapes.

Section 1
Life in the Family
1. SWC 9, 52
2. DD 126
3. DD 95, 96
4. SWC 160, 161
5. SWC 27, 28
6. HS 70, 71
7. DD 185
8. FF *Questions Parents Ask Most Frequently about Rearing Children*
9. SWC 162, 163
10. STTM 78, 79
11. HS 64, 65
12. FF *How to Save Your Marriage*
13. WWW 166, 167
14. DD 118-121 SWC 222
15. STTM 79-81
16. WWW 105-108
17. SWC 8

Section 2
Spiritual Training of Children
1. DD 179-181
2. SWC 57
3. STTM 75, 76
4. SWC 171, 172
5. FF *The Spiritual Training of Children*
6. SWC 174
7. STTM 73-75
8. DD 187, 188
9. HS 72, 73
10. SWC 56
11. SWC 141 FF *The Single Parent*
12. SWC 117
13. DD 43-46
14. STTM 146
15. DD 185, 186
16. HS 129
17. DD 181

18. STTM 81-85

Section 3
Education of Children
1. DD 162
2. DD 163, 164
3. HS 102, 103
4. DD 182, 183
5. DD 96, 97
6. DD 104, 105
7. DD 79-81
8. DD 164-166
9. SWC 185
10. SWC 185, 186

Section 4
Learning Problems in Childhood
1. From the *APA Monitor* (Washington, D.C.: American Psychological Association), vol. 7, no. 4, 1976, n.p.

2. SWC 48-50
3. SWC 161
4. DD 137
5. DD 159, 160
6. DD 136, 137
7. DD 139, 140
8. DD 160
9. DD 140, 141
10. DD 144, 145
11. DD 146-148
    HS 100
12. DD 103
13. DD 148
14. Further
    explanation of
    immediate
    reinforcement is
    provided on p. 178
    in this book.
15. DD 150-152
16. SWC 158-160

Section 5
**Sex Education at
Home and School**
1. DD 181, 182
2. DD 170, 171
3. DD 171
4. DD 175, 176
5. HS 133
6. DD 171-173
7. HS 141
8. HS 139, 141
9. DD 182

Section 6
**The Discipline of
Infants and Toddlers**
1. SWC 19
2. SWC 40
3. SWC 39
4. DD 90
   SWC 39, 40
5. SWC 41, 42
6. SWC 42, 44, 45, 50
7. SWC 70, 71
8. SWC 66, 67
9. FF *To Spank or Not
   to Spank*
10. SWC 47, 48
11. DD 61, 62
12. STTM 58-60, 70
13. SWC 52
14. SWC 53
15. DD 52, 53

Section 7
**Understanding the
Role of Discipline**
1. HS 96, 97
2. DD 52
3. DD 62
4. DD 33
5. SWC 182, 183
6. DD 25-27
7. DD 31
8. SWC 30
9. DD 55, 56
10. SWC 16-18
11. SWC 65, 66
12. SWC 176, 177
13. SWC 177, 178
14. SWC 179, 180
15. SWC 180, 181
16. SWC 181, 182
17. DD 46
18. DD 222-224
    SWC 171

Section 8
**The "How To" of
Discipline**
1. SWC 31-33
2. SWC 76-78
3. SWC 78, 83, 84
4. SWC 24, 25
5. DD 34
6. SWC 68
7. SWC 26, 27
8. SWC 99-101
9. DD 188, 189
10. SWC 23
11. SWC 115, 116
12. HS 98
13. DD 62
14. HS 98, 99
15. SWC 57-60
16. SWC 67, 68

Section 9
**Spankings: When,
How, and Why**
1. Marguerite and
   Willard Beecher,
   *Parents on the
   Run: A
   Commonsense
   Book for Today's
   Parents* (New York:
   Crown Publishers,
   Inc., 1955), 6-8.

Used by
permission.
2. SWC 73-76
3. John Valusek,
   Parade Magazine,
   February 6, 1977,
   n.p.
4. HS 95
5. SWC 34-38
6. SWC 33, 46, 47
7. DD 52
8. DD 58, 59
9. SWC 61
10. SWC 203-205

Section 10
Sibling Rivalry
1. SWC 126, 127
2. Beecher, n.p.
3. SWC 127, 128
4. SWC 128, 130
5. SWC 130
6. SWC 133-135
7. SWC 131-133
8. HS 88, 89
9. SWC 135, 136
10. SWC 135
11. HS 67, 68

Section 11
**Teaching Children to
Be Responsible**
1. SWC 25, 26
2. SWC 163, 164
3. DD 53, 54
4. HS 69
5. SWC 61, 62
6. SWC 113-115
7. SWC 69
8. DD 63-68
9. SWC 136
10. DD 71, 72
11. DD 73, 74
12. DD 74-77
13. DD 88-90
14. DD 78, 79
15. DD 84
16. DD 78, 84-86

Section 12
**Hyperactivity in
Children**
1. SWC 145-147
2. SWC 147, 148
3. SWC 148

4. SWC 149
5. SWC 150
6. *Ibid.*
7. SWC 151
8. SWC 151, 152
9. SWC 153
10. SWC 152, 153
11. SWC 154
12. SWC 155
13. SWC 155, 156
14. Renshaw, 118-120
15. SWC 156-158
16. SWC 160

Section 13
**Coping with
Adolescence**
1. HS 122
2. HS 122-125
3. PA 70, 71
4. HS 88
5. HS 138

6. HS 125
7. HS 128
8. HS 139
9. HS 115, 116
10. SWC 190-192
11. HS 79, 80
12. SWC 193, 194
13. HS 152-154
14. SWC 197-202
15. DD 90, 91
16. SWC 223
17. DD 181
18. HS 84, 85
19. DD 196
20. DD 194, 195
21. HS 161, 162
22. HS 129

Section 14
**Questions from
Adolescents**

1. PA 49
2. PA 69, 70
3. PA 28-31
4. PA 35, 36
5. PA 66-71
6. PA 71-77
7. PA 79
8. PA 79-86
9. PA 87, 88
10. PA 88-90

Section 15
**Television and
Violence**
1. HS 73, 74
2. FF *The Impact of
TV on Young Lives*
3. *Ibid.*
4. HS 165, 166
5. SWC 122, 123

QUESTION INDEX

GENERAL INDEX

BOOKS AND FILMS FOR THE FAMILY
by James Dobson

Dare to Discipline, Kingsway Publications 1971
Discipline While You Can, Kingsway Publications 1978
Hide or Seek, Hodder & Stoughton 1982
Preparing for Adolescence, Kingsway Publications 1982
Emotions: Can You Trust Them?, Hodder & Stoughton 1982
Man to Man About Women, Kingsway Publications 1976
Straight Talk to Men and Their Wives, Hodder & Stoughton 1981
Love Must Be Tough, Kingsway Publications 1984
Dr Dobson Answers Your Questions, Kingsway Publications 1983
  (Reissued in three separate volumes 1987)

Focus on the Family: a six-part film series
  distributed by International Films, 235 Shaftesbury Avenue,
  London WC2H 8EL

Dr Dobson Answers Your Questions about Marriage and Sexuality

by James Dobson

Dr James Dobson is highly respected as a leading expert on human psychology and Christian family life. Over the years he has been asked hundreds of questions, and this book sets out the answers he has given on a wide range of issues that affect the growth of the individual and the value of family life.

In *Marriage and Sexuality* Dr Dobson gives practical insights on —

— romance
— married life
— homemaking
— masculinity

— femininity
— sensuality
— menopause
— mid-life and beyond

James Dobson is President of Focus on the Family, a charitable body dedicated to the preservation of the home. For fourteen years he was Associate Clinical Professor of Pediatrics at the University of California School of Medicine, and was appointed by Presidents Jimmy Carter and Ronald Reagan to advise on family and juvenile matters. He is married with two children.

The contents of this book previously appeared in *Dr Dobson Answers Your Questions*.

Kingsway Publications

Preparing for Adolescence

by James Dobson

Uncertainty . . . pressure to conform . . . sexual worries . . . these are just a few of the new emotions and experiences that face young people today.

James Dobson is one of the most respected Christian writers on family life. He has written this book in the belief that it is better to *prepare* than *repair*. Young people between the ages of nine and fifteen are invited to read these pages and so face the upheaval of adolescence with their eyes open. Here they will find information, advice and—perhaps most important of all—*encouragement*.

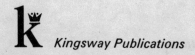

Kingsway Publications

Children at Risk

by David Porter

Our children—precious, inquisitive, vulnerable

This is an exciting age for children, where whole worlds of fantasy games, books and computers can be explored. Cinema and television excel in spectacular entertainment and stimulating education.

But there are risks.

David Porter, author and parent, takes us through some of the products and influences that are winning the minds of our children. While welcoming the wealth of creativity that so many bring, he sounds important warning notes for all those who wish to protect children from the nastier and more sinister elements of the market place. Finally we are alerted to the increasing physical danger our children face, as David looks at the unspoken risk of sexual abuse and the sale of drugs to under-fifteen-year-olds.

Parents and teachers will find this book a mine of information as well as a stirring manifesto for action. Brilliantly researched yet easy to read, it steers a course between the twin extremes of ill-advised panic and foolish complacency, showing us where the dangers lie and where we can tread the ground more confidently.

Children at Risk is not only a plea to manufacturers, retailers and local authorities to act responsibly; it is a reminder that we need to give our time, love and energy to our children, and share with them in the processes of education and play. To do anything less is to fail them where they need us most.

Kingsway Publications